A PRACTITIONER'S WAY FORWARD:

Terrorism Analysis

BY

DAVID BRANNAN
KRISTIN DARKEN
ANDERS STRINDBERG

An imprint of Agile Research and Technology, Inc.

Published in the United States by Agile Press,
an imprint of Agile Research and Technology, Inc. Salinas, CA

Printed in the United States of America
First printing, August 2014

ISBN 978-0-9830745-6-4

Illustrations by Kristin Darken & Matthew Prichard
Cover design by Matthew Prichard

info@agilepress.com
www.agilepress.com

CONTENTS

Preface

It is increasingly common that practitioners are called upon to engage in analysis related to homeland security. Law enforcement, the fire service, fusion centers, emergency management, public health, the Coast Guard, the National Guard, are among the disciplines in which professionals who are not analysts by training find themselves in need of analytical capabilities. They are searching for tools that are practical as well as intellectually rigorous, to allow them to effectively produce the analysis that they are called upon to deliver.

The so-called intelligence cycle is understood somewhat differently in the military and in law enforcement, but both models share some ground truths when it comes to analysis.[1] First, analysis is an integral component of a functioning intelligence cycle, especially long-term. Within that cycle, the purpose of analysis is to identify and shape the insights and new questions that will define future operational and policy needs. Second, while the steps of the cycle can be described separately—requirements; planning and direction; collection; processing and exploitation; analysis and production; dissemination and integration—they are not self-contained. In fact, they are collaborative, federated, and may "occur almost simultaneously."[2] Third, even though many departments, agencies, and commands have personnel specifically tasked with analysis, the task of analysis is also increasingly given to practitioners whose training and focus has been operational. It is plain to see that analysis is not some self-contained ivory

---

1   See "FBI—Intelligence Cycle," accessed 04/09/2013 at http://www.fbi.gov/about-us/
    intelligence/intelligence-cycle. Cf. Joint Chiefs of Staff, *Joint Publication 2.0: Joint
    Intelligence*, October 22, 2013, p. I-5, I-6.
2   Joint Chiefs of Staff, *Joint Publication 2.0*, p. I-5.

tower abstraction: the quality, accuracy, and timeliness of analysis are integral to the success of the homeland security mission, and practitioners are increasingly expected to be up to the task. Those charged with that responsibility need and deserve effective models and methods that allow them to get the job done. This volume seeks to fill that function.

We have spent nearly a decade working with students who are mid-career professionals within the disciplines identified above, teaching discourse analysis and analytical and critical thinking skills applied to the homeland security domain, at the Naval Postgraduate School's Center for Homeland Defense and Security (NPS/CHDS). Almost none of our students have entered into the program with specific expertise related to terrorism analysis, but many have nevertheless been called upon by their departments and agencies to respond to the growing need to more expertly understand the nature of terrorism and terrorist groups. What we have found is that these students learn to "do" analysis by getting comfortable with handling the two chief components of effective analysis: the analytical frameworks that surround any given subject matter, and the vast variety of sources from which they must draw the facts in order to produce analysis.

The FBI describes analysis as a process in which "information is logically integrated, put in context, and used to produce intelligence." The frames and methods explained in this book are intended to do exactly that by applying a structured method that is not only applicable to the full range of substate violent groups, but that is also repeatable and sound according to the canons of social science. This book is written to fill the gap that all too often exists between academia and practitioners; while academics will find the method useful, practitioners responsible for work related to terrorism, organized crime, gangs and transnational groups will benefit from the tools and insights generated within academia and translated here to their practical use.

We have written this book in a straightforward and conversational style, free from unnecessary jargon, and presented it in a user-friendly layout. In doing so, we used principles from cognitive science and learning theory, enabling the reader to more easily transfer what they learned here to their workplace. Because the book is designed to be instructional we have applied principles of instructional design throughout the book to help guide the reader to greater comprehension of the text.

- Each chapter begins with an overview and list of focus questions. These features help direct the reader by providing context for the chapter before launching directly into the text. They are designed to "set the stage" and provide an anchor to aid the reader in connecting to significant concepts within each chapter.
- "Just in time" learning is supported through set-aside boxes interspersed throughout the book. These boxes are used to provide definitions of key terms, supply additional information and insights, highlight core concepts, and distill complex theories into a simplified form.
- Throughout the book, conceptual learning is clarified and solidified through the use of numerous concrete and relevant examples - at key junctures thought-provoking questions are posed to the reader to further encourage active reading and application of new information and ideas.
- Visual learning is supported through the use of simple drawings. These drawings are intended to help the reader visualize a concept; "dual coding" engages both the visual and speech portions of our brains in order to yield greater understanding.
- Chapter summaries are included at the end of each chapter to help solidify learning by identifying central ideas and providing the reader with a brief review.

- The end of the book includes a list of references and additional resources instead of a traditional bibliography. This list of references is organized topically so readers interested in further studying foundational ideas presented in the book can easily find the resource of greatest interest to them.

In writing this book, and in learning how to teach analysis to practitioners, we have incurred a number of intellectual debts of gratitude. Professor Bruce Hoffman, Director of the Center for Security Studies and of the Security Studies Program at Georgetown University's Edmund A. Walsh School of Foreign Service has been profoundly important for our approach to understanding terrorism, through many years of professional advice, analytical insight, and friendship. Professor Philip Esler, Portland Chair of New Testament Studies at the University of Gloucestershire, has been similarly foundational for our understanding of the importance and utility of Social Identity Theory. The scholarship and creative genius of Steven McGriff, Professor-in-Residence at the Krause Center for Innovation, Foothill College, has been enlightening, and the ongoing support of Akron Innovations has been invaluable. Last, but certainly not least, we are also profoundly indebted to the successive cohorts of students who have gone through the Masters degree program at NPS/CHDS. We have learned from them a great deal about what works and what does not, about the tasks that face them in their respective departments, agencies, bureaus, and commands, and about the needs that accompany those tasks. This book is, in a very real sense, an attempt to respond to those needs.

Monterey, April 2014

Challenges to Analysis

Overview

Practitioners, analysts, and policy makers examining terrorism and terrorist groups face many challenges when striving to provide accurate analysis. This section identifies and outlines such potential challenges so that students of sub-state political violence can deal with these issues before they negatively impact their analysis, or ideally, are able to avoid them all together. A basic issue is bias; bias comes in many forms, most of which are not immediately apparent to the researcher. Bias has the ability to obscure or conceal important insights, thereby derailing accurate analysis. Another difficulty bias creates relates to research itself: finding reliable and accurate sources and knowing the difference between what is and is not relevant is difficult, but necessary for insightful analysis. Access and interaction are also significant and potentially difficult issues to consider in the analytical process. Finally, while the researcher may believe that attention to detail and critical analysis will compel decision makers to accept their analytical insights, not all analysis is well-received simply because it is accurate and insightful; the political realities that may impact a decision maker's consideration of your analysis are also discussed in this section.

Focus Questions:

- Why is it so difficult to analyze terrorism?
- How can cognitive/cultural bias hamper objective analysis?
- What external challenges does an analyst face in terms of access to reliable sources? What are some possible solutions to these problems?
- What effect does a dynamic environment have on your analysis?

Caution: "terrorist" is a loaded term! This is one of the most basic challenges that the analyst faces as he or she looks critically at terrorist organizations and their actions. Terrorism is a negatively connoted word that assumes, by definition, that those we have labeled as such are somehow "bad" or "dangerous." Politicians and media pundits love to use the word to define their enemies: the term is a succinct way of painting them as enemies of society. For instance, in 2010 Glenn Beck called Congresswoman Maxine Waters an "economic terrorist,"[1] and in 2011, Vice President Joseph Biden was accused of claiming that the Tea Party acted "like terrorists."[2] Clearly we are not going to ask you to have a favorable view of terrorism and terrorists, but rather to recognize that the use of the word is itself loaded with overwhelmingly negative assumptions, which is precisely why it is such a powerful term. To call someone a terrorist assumes guilt, therefore it contains its own built-in bias.[3] In her book *Teaching Critical Thinking*, bell hooks suggests that bias is the enemy of critical thought.[4] We agree with her assessment and further suggest it is equally the enemy of good analysis.

---

1   August 10, 2010 edition of the Glenn Beck Show.

2   http://www.politico.com/news/stories/0811/60421.html.

3   For instance, the American born U.S. citizen, Anwar al-Awaki was killed by the U.S. government without trial for being a terrorist and supporting terrorism. While the controversy may wage between politicos as to the legitimacy of killing a U.S. citizen labeled a terrorist, the action on the part of the government should give pause to analysts to consider the life and death importance of labeling, and the potential for harm that may come from analytical bias or assumptions. For the government's defense of taking this action against U.S. citizens, see, http://www.foxnews.com/us/2012/03/05/ap-source-holder-will-address-targeted-killings/.

4   bell hooks, *Teaching Critical Thinking: Practical Wisdom* (New York, NY: Routledge, 2010) pp. 103-110.

Bias is the enemy of critical thought

Hicks-Ho identifies 62 distinct cognitive biases that affect decision making. Many of those can also have a significant impact on our ability to critically analyze terrorist organizations and their actions.[5] Particularly

> **bias:** a tendency to believe that some people, ideas, etc., are better than others that usually results in treating some people unfairly.
>
> *(Merriam-Webster.com)*

dangerous to analysts are the so-called "bandwagon effect," adopting an analytical position because many others hold that position, and "confirmation bias," the tendency to look only for information that confirms one's pre-existing position. Both of these may lead an analyst toward conclusions that are politically or socially comfortable, but nevertheless may be completely false; looking for what others say is there or for what we hope to find, rather than what has not yet been uncovered or what we hope not to find, virtually guarantees that we will be led away from or induced to ignore relevant facts. Richard Betts highlighted this danger when he noted that there is almost always "some" evidence to support any position a person wants to take on a subject.[6] In relation to the dangers this poses to decision makers, he notes, "A wishful decision maker can fasten onto that half of an ambivalent analysis that supports his pre-disposition. A more objective official may escape this temptation, but may consider the estimate useless because it does not provide 'the answer.'"[7] Similarly, the Central Intelligence Agency's Center for the Study of Intelligence suggests, "It is important to suspend judgment while information is being assembled on each of the hypotheses. It is easy to form impressions about a hypothesis on the basis of very little information, but hard to

---

5   Danny Hope, *"Decision Making & Behavioral Biases,"* Accessed (July 21, 2012). http://oce. sph.unc.edu/mgmt_super/spring2012/hicks_ho2_cognitive_biases.pdf.

6   Richard Betts, "Analysis, War, and Decision: Why Intelligence Failures Are Inevitable", *World Politics,* Vol. 31, No. 1, October 1978.

7   Ibid., p. 71.

change an impression once it has taken root."[8] Bias may influence whether or not you perceive an action as terrorism.

National tastes, priorities, and intellectual fashions are just some types of biases that affect whether one considers a group a terrorist organization that must be defeated or an environmental activist group that deserves public support. Paul Watson and his crew from the Sea Shepherd Conservation Society—now famous from their hit TV show on the Animal Planet network, "Whale Wars"—present an interesting case study.[9] Some have suggested that the program inappropriately supports terrorists, as the Sea Shepherds' actions fall under a formal definition of terrorism.[10] The Sea Shepherds tactics have included disabling whaling vessels in the harbor, using limpet mines to blow holes in their hulls, throwing bottles with butyric acid onto other vessels, and ramming other vessels at sea. They have targeted, among others, Japanese whaling ships and the Japanese whaling industry, although these attacks have further strengthened Japanese support for whaling in Japan.[11] At the same time, much of the American viewing public appears willing to accept the attacks as legitimate because they view the Sea Shepherds' actions as saving endangered animals—something different from terrorism. Analysts asked

---

8   http://www.cia.gov/csi/books/19104/art17.html.

9   http://animal.discovery.com/tv/whale-wars/sea-shepherd or http://planetgreen.discovery. com/videos/focus-earth-2-saving-the-whales-is-this-eco-terrorism.html for an interview with Watson addressing the question directly.

10 For an interesting discussion of this issue see Gerry Nagtzaam and Pete Lentini, "Vigilantes on the High Seas?: The Sea Shepherds and Political Violence," *Terrorism and Political Violence.* Vol. 20, No. 1 (2007) pp.110-133. Proponents of this understanding of terrorism suggest that the Sea Shepherds' actions meet the criteria for a terrorist group; 1) they are a sub-national group, B) using force or the fear of force, C) against non-combatants, D) to instill fear in those beyond the victims directly attacked, E) in an effort to change political or social structures. In this understanding of the Sea Shepherds' actions against Japanese whalers, the essential tenants defining terrorism are met in their clashes with whaling vessels.

11 Jeff Kingston, "Whaling Whoppers Debunked," *The Japan Times*, April 25, 2010, p.11, The article claims that because whale meat was part of a Japanese school lunch program from the end of WWII until the early 1960s, it is nationalistically nostalgic for some Japanese baby boomers. Attacks against the Japanese and other countries have often consisted of collisions between the Sea Shepherds' ships and whaling vessels.

Biases and Fallacies

Because we are humans, and not machines, our ability to process information is not flawless. It is, however, surprisingly predictable, a fact that we are increasingly aware of, thanks to years of research conducted by social psychologists. The goal of understanding and identifying bias types and traits is to build a better analytical product upon which effective decisions can be based. The list below highlights a few to consider in your own analysis.

Anchoring: the tendency to rely too heavily on, or "anchor" oneself to, one trait or piece of information when making decisions.

Backfire Effect: when people react to disconfirming evidence by strengthening their beliefs.

Bandwagon Effect: the tendency to do (or believe) things because many other people do (or believe) the same.

Confirmation Bias: the often unconscious act of referencing only those perspectives that strengthen our pre-existing views, while simultaneously ignoring or dismissing opinions that threaten our world view.

Clustering Illusion: the tendency to see patterns where none actually exist.

Fallacy of Composition: arises when a conclusion is drawn about a whole based on the features of its constituents when, in fact, no justification is provided for the inference. Its opposite is the fallacy of division, whereby characteristics of a whole are assumed to be equally characteristic of all its constituents.

Ingroup Bias: preferential treatment given to those who are perceived to be members of one's own group. Its opposite is outgroup bias, the tendency to be more critical of those who are not part of one's ingroup.

Neglect of Probability: the tendency to completely disregard probability when making a decision under uncertainty.

Observational Selection Bias: suddenly noticing things that were not noticed previously and, as a result, wrongly assuming that the frequency has increased.

Outcome Bias: the tendency to judge a decision by its eventual outcome rather than by the quality of decision at the time it was made.

Selective Perception: when expectations affect perception.

Status Quo Bias: the tendency to prefer when things stay relatively the same.

Zero-risk Bias: preference for reducing a small risk to zero over a greater reduction of a larger risk.

(Danny Hope, "Decision Making & Behavioral Biases")

to consider the actions of these types of groups must stop and consider their own biases and how they might impact their analysis.

Bias works on multiple levels. Sarah Beebe and Randy Pherson have suggested that a biased mindset contains insufficient "mental bins" to counteract the "cognitive ruts" in which our analysis is often situated.[12] So, not only does bias lead us in the wrong direction, it actually deprives us of the means to prevent and overcome our tendency to think about certain issues in different ways. A way to avoid this trap – to circumvent the dangers imposed by bias – is to use a structured method for thinking about the complex and challenging issues surrounding terrorists and terrorism. In a nutshell, that is the goal of this book. The method we suggest is one that allows for sufficient "mental bins" into which information can be placed and processed, while at the same time structuring our analysis based a model that forces us out of our "cognitive ruts," therefore minimizing bias-based errors.

Biased Mind   Structured Methodology

Distorted or inaccurate analysis is potentially more dangerous than a complete lack of analysis because it misdirects counter-terrorism efforts by misconstruing the scope, purposes, alliances, or even the identity of different terrorists and terrorist groups. For instance, stereotypes and other generalized assumptions might lead analysts to believe that there are substantive operational

---

12 Sarah Miller Beebe and Randall H. Pherson, *How Do Cognitive Pitfalls Limit Our Ability to Anticipate Rare Events?* (2009 Pherson Associates, LLC.), pp. 5, 3.

or strategic links between groups where none actually exist. If our analytical assumptions suggest that groups are the same, when in fact they are not, it can have a negative impact in a number of ways. For instance, if we were to assume that all Salafi groups are also terrorist groups, we might run the risk of pushing nonviolent Salafis toward violence.[13]

Using an American example, we could look to racially-based theology in the United States. The Aryan Nations is a well-known religiously-motivated violent group, professing what is known as "Christian Identity" theology. Their collision with U.S. law enforcement is typically caused when the group takes illegal actions in an effort to bring about some change to racial, political, and social situations in the U.S. and elsewhere. In 2000, the Idaho-based group was crippled when the Southern Poverty Law Center (SPLC) won a $6.3 million judgment against it. The SPLC had brought a legal suit following an attack by the Aryan Nation guards on a mother and her son who had driven past the group's compound.[14] As you can see in the footnotes below, the group is clearly identified as an Identity theology group. This label is correct, but it might lead an analyst to deduce falsely that all Identity theology-based groups are similarly violent or prone to terrorism. This is known as the "fallacy of composition": the assumption that what is true for one part of something is therefore true about all others parts ("one apple is rotten, therefore I can assume that all apples are rotten"). On the contrary, there are many Identity theology groups that reject both violent action and breaking the law. As such, they do not really fit into the same terrorist category as the Aryan Nations. The Church of Israel in Schell City, MO, and Mission

---

13 See for instance, Mark Woodward, Inayah Rohmaniyah, Ali Amin and Diana Coleman, "Muslim Education, Celebrating Islam and Having Fun As Counter-Radicalization Strategies in Indonesia," *Perspectives on Terrorism*, Vol 4, No 4 (2010), Accessed at, http:://www.terrorismanalysts.com/pt/index.php/pot/article/view/114/html.

14 See for instance, http://www.splcenter.org/get-informed/intelligence-files/groups/aryan-nations, or, http://www.adl.org/learn/ext_us/aryan_nations.asp?xpicked=3&item=an or for a non-watch dog perspective see, http://www.start.umd.edu/start/data_collections/tops/terrorist_organization_profile.asp?id=29.

to Israel of Scottsbluff, NE, are both Identity theology groups, yet neither is violent.[15] Though their racial theology is contrary to mainstream ideas and values, these non-violent Identity adherents nevertheless follow a religious belief system protected by the Constitution in the same way that other non-violent groups are protected. Distinguishing between those who are violent and those who are not, regardless of their politics, is extremely important for the discerning analyst.

In analysis, just as during the investigative process, details are crucial. Indeed, if responder communities are provided with inaccurate analysis, it may lead to actions that violate Constitutional rights.[16] When policy makers are given inaccurate analysis, bad policy decisions are made that can produce ill effects of all sorts. Analysts should strive to avoid the snares of prejudiced, or mistaken assumptions. It is often impossible to disentangle analytical inaccuracy from policy failures, as analysis and decision-making are ideally dynamic, rather than sequential, processes.[17]

Sources

All sources are not created equal. Many first responders who have been involved with news media during or after an incident can attest to how seemingly straightforward information is spun in certain ways, becoming distorted once in the hands of a media outlet. A recurring question among practitioners is, how can the media's presentation of information stray so far from the experience of those who had first-hand knowledge of a given event?

---

15 See, David W. Brannan, Violence, *Terrorism and the Role of Theology: Repentant and Rebellious Christian Identity* at, http://research-repository.st-andrews.ac.uk/handle/10023/342 for an academic handling of the various groups detailed here.

16 An example of this danger was recently debated in the public media because of the surveillance of Muslims by NYPD. See, http://www.msnbc.msn.com/id/46718217/ns/us_news/t/nypd-surveillance-muslims-popular-it-legal/#.T20q-3iqXpA.

17 Richard Betts, "Analysis, War, and Decision: Why Intelligence Failures Are Inevitable", *World Politics*, Vol. 31, No. 1, October 1978, pp. 66-67.

When information is presented – anywhere, anytime, almost without exception – it is given within one or several frames.[18] Frames profoundly shape what we take away from information presented to us—it is what they are designed to do. Frames provide context. They may be political, cultural, or social, but the function of frames is always to establish the context through which we understand information being presented to us. As such, frames impact the associations we make and the conclusions we draw about the

> **framing:** selecting and highlighting some facets of events or issues, and making connections among them so as to promote a particular interpretation, evaluation, and/or solution.
> (Robert M. Entman, *Projections of Power: Framing News, Public Opinion and U.S. Foreign Policy* (p.5)

information. Obvious examples of frames can be found every day in cable news shows. For instance, MSNBC is known to apply one kind of political frame to its reporting, while FOX News is known to apply a very different kind of frame.[19] If you listen to information presented on any number of topics by these two channels, even covering the same event on the same day, you may come away with very different understandings of the same story. This is because the networks impose two very different frames. These political frames can also be seen quite clearly through the way that different political parties "spin" the same issues in very different ways.

We also come across other, perhaps less obvious frames, such as religious, cultural, regional, and ethnic frames. These all serve the same basic function: to create boundaries for, and give context to, any given topic. In other words, they affect the way in which you understand a story. This is hugely important for analysts because when we analyze terrorism and terrorist groups, every data point

---

18 For a more complete handling of how information is framed as it relates to news, public opinion and U.S. foreign policy, see Robert M. Entman, *Projections of Power*, (Chicago, University of Chicago Press, 2004).

19 See http://www.msnbc.msn.com/. See also http://www.foxnews.com/.

we collect comes to us within one or several frames that are designed to influence our understanding of that data point. Not knowing what frames surround our data point—taking data at face value—is dangerous to analysis. However, if we are aware of these frames we can use data in its proper context; it is the analyst's equivalent of situational awareness.

As an analyst, you need to get beyond the report and seek the original sources of information in order to ensure the reliability of your analysis and to be able to own it with confidence. Analysts must recognize that the government also practices framing: government reports are simply events or issues that have been fitted to the government's preferred frame. The same is true of press conferences, speeches, official interviews, media appearances, and so on. Everyone, friend and foe alike, engages in framing.

If you simply accept as fact all of the information the the U. S. government provides—at its many levels and from its many branches—you may find yourself struggling to reconcile contradictory viewpoints. Consider the public statements made by Ambassador Susan Rice following the attack on the U.S. Consulate in Benghazi, Libya in 2012.[20] Four Americans were killed in the attack, including Ambassador Chris Stevens, and it occurred in the midst of regional unrest related to an amateurish film depicting the life of the Prophet Mohammad, *The Innocence*

---

20 Taken from the US Embassy website in Libya; http://iipdigital.usembassy.gov/st/english/texttrans/2012/09/20120912135826.html?CP.rss=true#axzz26GF576Q5. Accessed online 12-13-12.

of Muslims, which was available in part on YouTube. [21] On various Sunday news shows, Ambassador Rice discussed the attack using unclassified information that suggested that the Benghazi attack was related to broader regional protests against the video. Later it was revealed that she had been aware of classified information showing that the attack was unrelated to the demonstrations.[22] One might claim that Ambassador Rice used the YouTube video to frame the Benghazi attack, but that this frame later proved irrelevant. Indeed, her use of that first ill-fitting frame was later turned against her in a political effort to derail her nomination as Secretary of State.

Both the classified and the unclassified accounts of the Benghazi attacks were "government information," yet they appear to have contained contradictory information leading to divergent accounts of what happened and why. Political frames, intelligence frames, and national security frames all demanded that the same set of facts should be presented in different ways—that is, set in reference to different surrounding explanatory factors. Though all of the perspectives were presented by U.S. government sources, they were different government sources with various institutional objectives. Relying on government sources without understanding how and why different forces within the government may wish to present information using particular frames can easily compromise analytical insight and accuracy.

One way to manage bias and avoid inaccurate assumptions is to use trusted sources of information. This may seem self-evident but, in some positions, an employer provides information to an analyst assuming that he or she has everything needed in order to work out the analysis. This may not be true, even if the information in question is classified or obtained outside of open

---

21 http://www.youtube.com/watch?v=mjoa3QazVy8&bpctr=1369769701. Accessed online 5-28-13.

22 *The Economist*, "Why They Won't Calm Down," http://www.economist.com/node/21562960 print edition, September 15, 2012. Accessed online 12-13-12.

sources.[23] First, it is false to assume that simply because information is classified, it is therefore more useful than open source material; in both classified and open source materials, the nature and quality of the source determines usefulness. Second, and more importantly, even classified information needs to be understood within its relevant frames—that is, it needs to be understood in context. Analysts need to push for outside verification as much as possible in order to corroborate and authenticate data and assumptions. As we discussed above, poorly grounded assumptions are dangerous to effective analysis.

It might be ideal for analysts to obtain and vet their source information themselves, first hand. While not always possible, obtaining primary source material is rarely impossible. Nevertheless, vetting sources is a lot of work: identifying the frames used in the presentation of the message,

A **primary source** is an original object or document -- the raw material or first-hand information. It hasn't been interpreted, analyzed, condensed or changed.

A **secondary source** is something written about a primary source. Secondary sources include comments on, interpretations of, or discussions about the original material. You can think of secondary sources as second-hand information.

(Adapted from: Old Dominion University Library, Ithaca College Library)

finding gaps in information, ascertaining the accuracy of translations, and so forth. This is necessary whether one is dealing with primary source material (e.g. an unedited statement by a terrorist leader) or some secondary source (e.g. a news report about a terrorist attack). It can be both time-consuming and tedious, and finding high quality sources about a region, people, group, or incident can be difficult depending on the circumstances. Language and cultural differences can further introduce elements of uncertainty that may or may not be accounted for in reporting.

---

23 For instance, information obtained legally during a criminal investigation.

A particularly famous and politically important example of such a cultural misunderstanding occurred in 1956. After a policy speech at the Polish Embassy in Moscow, Soviet Premier Nikita Khrushchev argued for communism's superiority over capitalism, saying to Western ambassadors, "We will bury you." The statement caused a global stir. The Suez Canal crisis in Egypt was ongoing, the superpower arms race was in its early stages and the Soviets had recently completed their first successful test of a hydrogen bomb. Against this background, U.S. media outlets uniformly reported the statement as a threat from a dangerous enemy; as such, it fed the spiraling arms and space races.[24] While the global political context was significant, what the reporters (and consequently their readership) missed was that Khrushchev's remark was meant to assert the vitality of communism and the fragility of capitalism. Khrushchev's statement was not a threat, but a prediction about which socio-economic system would outlast the other. Understood in its immediate context, Khrushchev was in fact using a Russian idiom that might have been better translated as "We will be present at your burial." However, the charged geopolitical context and the reporters' assumptions drowned out the immediate context of the remark and it instead fueled decades of increased political tension.

Some analysts address the challenge of obtaining source material by relying on websites and subscription services specializing in providing primary source information on terrorism to counter-terrorism practitioners. Rather than solving the problem, however, these services actually present several new challenges that are difficult to overcome if one's website of choice or subscription service is allowed to become singularly authoritative. Many of the terrorism intel services are for-profit entities. This is important because there are two common and important aspects of such enterprises. First, each source reflects the editorial overlay of its owners, which means that the material is likely to be selected and edited to reflect their personal of self-interested opinions. Second, the material

---

24 *Time Magazine*, November 26, 1956. Accessed on http://www.time.com/time/magazine/article/0,9171,867329,00.html.

is designed to draw in customers: in some cases, this means overstating groups' capacities, threat levels, and so forth. Because such frames are usually carefully hidden from the subscriber's view, they are difficult to discern and even more troublesome to overcome. Nevertheless, ultimately the analyst must establish his or her own frame in order to accurately assess a group or interpret an event.

Access and interaction

Access and interaction present formidable challenges for researchers who want to effectively analyze terrorism, especially when the analyst is a federal, state, local, or tribal government employee, or a student conducting academic research.[25] Again, as analysts, we want to be as close to the source for information as possible. This is not only due to the necessity of source verification, but also because the subjects of our research are groups of people; as such, they are subjects rather than objects.[26] Ongoing access to and interaction with the subject of our analysis gives us analytical insight that documents, transcripts, and secondary source information cannot provide alone.

Sometimes access and interaction manifests as a language barrier: how do you interact with a community if they speak a language you do not understand? What if the attack or group that you are asked to analyze is located in a country to which you cannot travel or in which you have no contacts? Regardless of such difficulties, your employer may still call upon you to provide analysis, with or without proper access. The question then becomes whether these difficulties can be overcome.

---

25 One must exercise caution with whom and how one interacts with groups deemed inappropriate by one's government agency, employer, or institutional review board process. There are clear guidelines which must not be exceeded. Each practitioner must take care to follow appropriate institutional rules and regulations.

26 David W. Brannan, Philip F. Esler and N.T. Anders Strindberg, "Talking to Terrorists: Towards an Independent Analytical Framework for the Study of Violent Substate Activism," *Studies in Conflict and Terrorism*, 24.1 (January/February 2001), pp. 3-24.

Boots on the Ground
David Brannan

In 2003 and 2004 I worked in Iraq as the Director of Security Policy in the Coalition Provisional Authority's Ministry of Interior. Though I myself did not speak Arabic, I was called upon to interact with Arabic speakers and documents on a regular basis. In these cases, the use of a translator was marginally helpful but also exposed potential weaknesses and dangers to analysis. The contracted translators were not known or trusted by some of the groups with which we worked, and we often wondered what was or was not actually being said during our discussions. Because of the sensitive position these translators held as Iraqi nationals employed by the USG, but not from the group with which we were interacting, we constantly looked for validation of our analysis. As a solution, we hired two non-Iraqi Western CPA employees who were fluent Arabic speakers as assistants. They attended meetings with us, the groups we were interacting with, and our translators without divulging their language capabilities, and we were slowly able to gain the access and interaction we needed. The resolution did not happen overnight and this particular method might not always work in other situations, but the point is that if access becomes a priority, you need to find a solution that enables you to achieve it within your particular circumstances.

Two or more possibilities present themselves. One is simply to state the limitations in the analysis and why those limitations occur. This way you make it clear that although decision makers relying on your analysis can gain insight from your work, they cannot expect perfect insight into every situation. Alternately, if the issue, group, or action is critical to the long-term efforts of your organization, a strategy for overcoming these limitations should be devised. Access to language expertise, developing relationships of trust with those who have insider access, and securing corroborated expertise may then become top priorities.

Is all analysis received equally?

Analysis of terrorism and terrorist groups is not done in a vacuum. Local, state, tribal, and national government entities are often those who request analysis, but they are subject to very real political constraints and demands from a range of actors. Such an environment affects how analysis is received: what may be analytically sound and accurate may not be politically acceptable or prudent. Political, religious, and ideological groups and communities that you may be called upon to analyze may be cast and recast in different political lights, sometimes daily, for seemingly unrelated (or even entirely unknown) political reasons. This is often the 800 lb gorilla in the room: the responder community knows the "ground truth" about an organization but runs up against a political landscape that is unable or unwilling to accept a particular analysis, or may even push to influence an analyst to find results favorable to a given political constituency.

For instance, this was the perception of Michael Scheuer, who anonymously wrote *Through Our Enemies' Eyes*, in which he described his conviction that political frames had derailed his analysis-based warnings while he served as an CIA analyst, working on al-Qaeda and bin Laden.[27] In 2004 he left the

---

27 See, Anonymous, *Through our Enemies' Eyes: Osama bin Laden, Radical Islam, and the Future of America*, (Washington DC, Brassey's, 2002).

CIA in frustration because, as he perceived it, politics were keeping the U.S. from comprehending the threat presented by bin Laden, and from taking appropriate military action in response to that threat. He made key predictions on the basis of critical analysis prior to 9-11, and it is the perception of the present authors that Scheuer paid a heavy price for his unbending analytical courage—including changing his career prematurely. Political frames regularly determine whether or not an analytical product will be accepted.

Another important challenge to analysis is the fact that social phenomena are not static, and that analysis must be updated regularly. The analyst must have the courage to recognize changes in political, contextual, and group dynamics that can alter conclusions, even if this means that his or her own prior analysis is no longer valid. Contextual considerations change continuously and analysis should account for and reflect this dynamism. This can be problematic for researchers who become wedded to their initial analysis and are not willing to adapt to a constantly changing landscape, a problem often seen in academic settings: a researcher makes an early discovery, publishes that position, and then spends significant effort protecting his or her position against attacks from colleagues; the position, not its accuracy, becomes what matters.

Chapter Summary:

- The term terrorist (or terrorism) is a loaded term, with built in bia presumes guilt.

- Bias is the enemy of critical thought and objective analysis.

- Analysts need to be cognizant of bias when conducting critical analysis.

- Analysts benefit from the use of structured methods to guide their analysis and force them out of cognitive ruts that inhibit objective analysis.

- Inaccurate analysis can be more damaging than no analysis at all, leading to misdirection and poor policy decisions with significant negative impacts for homeland security practitioners.

- Analysts must do their utmost to ensure the accuracy of source material, and try to get it from as close to the research subject as possible.

- Analysts must allow their analysis to develop and track with changing realities on the ground.

2

Thinking about Terrorism

Overview

This chapter considers what an appropriate framework for analyzing terrorism and terrorist groups might look like. Terrorism's immorality as a tactic often means that we respond emotionally to its use; while this tells us something about ourselves, it yields very little useful information about the terrorists using it. Our frameworks for critically analyzing the complex and diverse political challenges posed by terrorism require systematic evaluation, not just moral revulsion. We will discuss some common analytical methods, many of which were carried over from the state-centric geopolitical environment of the Cold War. Instead of conceptualizing terrorists as "psychopaths," we are challenged to think of them as rational political actors—a difficult framework to accept, because it suggests that terrorists are fundamentally not so different from "normal" people.

Focus Questions:

- Why is a structured framework so important to practitioners analyzing terrorism?

- What does a psychological explanatory model of terrorism suggest about the root causes of terrorism?

- What are the limitations of these models?

- How does the strategic (or rational) choice model account for terrorism, and what problems arise within this model?

- What does the Social Identity Theory (SIT) framework provide that the traditional theories and models described in this chapter do not?

How do you think about terrorism? On the surface this may appear a strange question; most people tend to see terrorism simply as an evil to be defeated.[1] Certainly the killing and maiming of innocent non-combatants—an essential element of this type of political violence—should be met with disdain as well as forceful counteraction.[2] But is moral outrage a helpful framework for understanding the nature of this, or any, threat? Our moral compass helps us know why we fight terrorists, but it is not really useful for figuring out why terrorists engage in terrorism, much less how they do it or how we can more effectively defend against it. In this handbook, we argue that there are certain analytical theories, processes, and frameworks that can help non-experts in the field understand the underpinnings, motivations, methods, and goals of terrorists. Once you have a greater understanding of terrorism and terrorists, you can then provide more precise and therefore more useful analysis to decision makers. Morality may be the starting point for our outrage, but it is not a suitable foundation or framework for analysis. If our analysis is to be used for developing effective and systematic government policy and action against groups and organizations engaging in terrorism, our task must be to rationally and

---

1   See Christopher Hewitt, *Understanding Terrorism in America: From the Klan to al-Qaeda* (London and New York: Routledge, 2003), pp.106-113 for a review of U.S. public opinion and media coverage through 2001. See also, Benjamin Netanyahu, *Fighting Terrorism* (New York: Farrar, Straus and Giroux, 2001) for a common view of terrorism as an immoral action to be defeated.

2   Whether it is the six-point outline for how to "deal with terrorism" as found in Louis Richardson's, *What Terrorists Want: Understanding the Enemy, Containing the Threat*, (New York: Random House Trade Paperbacks, 2006), the policy focused strategic perspective of Philip B. Heymann's, *Terrorism and America: A Commonsense Strategy for a Democratic Society*, (Cambridge: MIT Press, 1998), or perhaps the moral outrage thesis put forward by David Frum and Richard Perle, in *An End to Evil: How to Win the War on Terror*, (New York: Random House, 2003), the focus of much of the respected counterterrorism literature is on terrorism's immorality and its status as something our society needs to fight against and defeat.

methodically examine facts.[3]

This difficult task requires the student of terrorism to move beyond the media sound bites and moral or patriotic slogans, applying arduous research to difficult and complex social and political situations. This can be hard work; it requires significant effort and should not be taken lightly. Yet a person need not be an expert in languages or cultures, or even a so-called "terrorism expert" in order to provide helpful analysis related to terrorism. Terrorists' actions may be immoral, but they are also, contrary to popular opinion, quite rational. As a result, they can be understood and countered using careful analysis. To accomplish this, one must systematically use rigorous analytical methods and models. We will go into more detail about what we mean by this later in the chapter, but for now it is important to note that these models are essentially frames within which the analyst examines groups or events.

As we noted in the previous chapter, frames are perspectives that affect our understanding of certain information or situations. When an analyst uses analytical models, he or she considers a given phenomenon within different frames in order to better and more fully understand the causes, reasons, motivations, alignments, and so forth, that led to the particular phenomenon's occurrence. Different frames highlight or emphasize different factors and features. While good analysis does not require a person to be a specialist, effort is required to become a competent generalist who is able to use the tools required for the task at hand.

Terrorism studies, models, and interpretations

Much of terrorism literature lacks the theoretical frameworks that are needed to support or produce accurate analysis. While there is certainly solid scholarship

---

3   Modern terrorism is typically thought of as possessing these four components: a) the threat or use of violence, b) intimidating those beyond the immediate audience of the violence, c) directed toward civilians, and d) intended to impact the social or political landscape.

within the field, the often pseudo-empirical and "quasi-gritty" nature of what is written in the name of counter-terrorism and terrorism studies lacks truly rigorous methodology. This becomes extremely important to students, analysts, decision makers, and others who want to use the material to produce analysis capable of standing up to intense scrutiny. An analyst who is developing skills related to critical analysis of insurgent, terrorist, and criminal organizations must not fear methodology, but embrace it and become adept at using it.

> **Methodology:** a set of methods, rules, or ideas that are important in a science or art : a particular procedure or set of procedures.
> *(Merriam-Webster.com)*

When terrorism studies emerged as a distinct field of study in the early to mid-1970s, there were some efforts to apply general theories of political violence to terrorism, led by, among others, T.R. Gurr.[4] By the late 1970s, these theories had generally fallen out of favor with the terrorism studies community and were replaced by more specifically terrorism-focused approaches. These models, in turn, proved problematic for a number of reasons. Most importantly, the array of sociological, communicative, psychological, and power political interpretations of terrorism paid little attention to social realities on the ground, and could also only partially account for different phenomena. Scholars often interpreted terrorism in ways that may have seemed morally appropriate, but that were often analytically imprecise, inaccurate, dubious, or simply useless—and above all, not based in any significant way on primary research, or research that included first-hand contact with the primary sources.[5]

---

4   T. R. Gurr, *Why Men Rebel*, (Princeton, NJ: Princeton University Press, 1970); see also his 'Some Characteristics of Political Terrorism in the 1960s,' in M. Stohl (ed.) *The Politics of Terrorism* (New York: M. Dekker, 1979), pp. 23-45.

5   For a comprehensive stocktaking and critique of the first decade of terrorism studies, see Alex P. Schmid, Albert J. Jongman et al, *Political Terrorism: A Research Guide to Concepts, Theories, Databases and Literature* (Amsterdam: North Holland Publishing, 1983).

Context

There are numerous definitions, and much debate, about the meaning and function of context. Here are two definitions that may be helpful:

1. Context is "a set of recognized conventions" that give objects a particular meaning. (Dilley, p. 18)

2. That which environs the object of interest and helps by its relevance to explain it." (Scharfstein, p. 1)

Determining relevant contexts may be the hardest task when analyzing terrorism. Terrorists use violence as a form of communication, which means that contexts are always essential. Also, while one context may be more important than another, there is almost never just a single context that is relevant to understanding an act of terrorism or a terrorist group. But which ones are relevant? And how do different contexts relate to one another? Analysts must consider:

- Historical contexts
- Political contexts
- Economic contexts
- Cultural contexts

Other aspects also need to be considered:

- The internal context of the terrorist group
- The context of the terrorist group's wider constituency
- The context of the target or target audience

Figuring out which of these contexts (and others) are relevant sets *good analysis* apart from *poor analysis*.

To think on:

We know that politicians say and promise different things in different contexts; that the audience, election cycle, popularity ratings and other needs and pressures impact what they say and how they say it.

Is there a reason to expect terrorist leaders to behave differently?

Because of the violent and dangerous nature of the research subject, many scholars have felt justified replacing primary research with a physically, politically, and morally safe distance from their research subjects. Historical and technical descriptions of terrorist groups and actions, devoid of theoretical frameworks, have also been common.[6] The obviously immoral nature of politically-motivated attacks against non-combatants, the core of terrorist violence, has allowed complacent researchers to make their claims about terrorism-related phenomena based solely on experience or morality. As a result, much of terrorism studies literature since its inception appears starkly different from the rigorous and research-based academic work that is typically expected from the social science disciplines. Theorizing terrorism has been problematic, not only as a consequence of the diverse nature of the groups and individuals categorized as "terrorists," but perhaps primarily because of the prevalence of unrealistic and inappropriate models and research conducted outside of proper context.

6   For instance the publication, *The Counter Terrorist* which purports to be a "Journal for Law Enforcement, Intelligence & Special Operations Professionals," and is a popular publication targeting the responder community, presents interesting and colorful articles and pictures, but lacks any analytically relevant framework. Absent such a framework the basic question is: how can analysts support and defend their findings?

Of all the interpretations that have defined the field of terrorism studies since the late 1970s, psychological and power political interpretations by far have dominated the literature. It should be noted that various theoretical approaches are often patched together without regard for analytical coherence.

Terrorism: abnormal psychopathology?

For many years, popular explanatory models suggested that terrorist violence was the outworking of psychopathology or some compulsion specific to the individual terrorist.[7] These psychological models, proposed by notables within terrorism studies such as Jerrold Post and Walter Laqueur, were in fact prominent within the field of terrorism studies until quite recently. The influence of this model is apparent in a 1999 U.S. government report titled "Who Becomes a Terrorist and Why."[8] The report, used as an authoritative text following al-Qaeda's 9/11 attacks, reinforced the perception that terrorists are mentally ill and that "terrorists are fanatics and fanaticism frequently makes for cruelty and sadism."[9]

Early Psychological Model

Research in the areas of psychopathology and psychoanalysis, however, have largely discounted the long-standing assertions that terrorists differ psychologically from the rest of us. Earlier and largely preliminary research may have indicated that individuals engage in terrorism because of self-destructive

---

7   Jerrold M. Post, "'Terrorist Psycho-Logic: Terrorist Behavior as a Product of Psychological Forces," in Walter Reich (ed.), *Origins of Terrorism: Psychologies, Ideologies, Theologies, States of Mind* (New York et alibi: Cambridge University Press, 1990), pp. 25-40.

8   Rex A. Hudson et al, *Who Becomes a Terrorist and Why: The 1999 Government Report on Profiling Terrorists*, (Guildford, Connecticut: The Lyons Press, 2001).

9   Ibid., p.40, 41.

urges,[10] fantasies of cleanliness,[11] disturbed emotions combined with problems with authority and the Self,[12] and inconsistent mothering.[13] Some continue to argue for the utility of such approaches.[14] However, after three decades of intense research there is still no actual evidence to support the argument that terrorists in general are psychologically deviant or defective. As such, to continue pursuing this approach is simply an analytical waste of time. Konrad Kellen has noted that psychological interpretations of terrorist violence "may or may not be accurate [in particular cases, but] lack general applicability."[15] That is to say, just like any given person on the street, any given terrorist may have psychiatric or psychopathological problems, but there is no data to support the assumption that terrorists generally suffer such problems. In fact, Clark McCauley shows how this basic approach can be reformulated in a way that does provide useful information, suggesting, "The psychology behind terrorist violence is normal psychology, abnormal only in the intensity of the group dynamics that link cause with comrades."[16]

In short, individual psychology is not an explanation of terrorism; it is rather an analytical trap that seems appealing because it looks scientific. It is comforting because it places a safe distance between "us" and "them"—"they" must be fundamentally different, fundamentally flawed in order to carry out

---

10 Wilhelm F. Kasch, "Terror: Bestandteil einer Gesellshaft ohne Gott?" in H. Geissler (ed.) *Der Weg in die Gewalt* (Munich: Olzog, 1978), pp. 52-68.

11 R. S. Frank as quoted by Gerhard Schmidtchen, "Bewaffnete Heilelehren" in ibid., p. 49.

12 W. Salewski as quoted in Z. Zofka, *Denkbare Motive und mögliche Aktionsformen eines Nukleärterrorismus* (Essen: Auge, 1981), p. 27.

13 Jonas as quoted in E. F. Mickolus, *The Literature of Terrorism* (Westport, CT: Greenwood Press, 1980), p. 361.

14 Joan Lachkar, "The Psychological Make-up of a Suicide Bomber," *Journal of Psychohistory*, No. 20 (2002), pp. 349-367.

15 Konrad Kellen, "Terrorists—What are They Like? How some Terrorists Describe their World and Actions" in Brian M. Jenkins (ed.) *Terrorism and Beyond: An International Conference on Terrorism and Low-Level Conflict* (Santa Monica, CA: Rand, 1982), p. 126.

16 See Clark McCauley, "The Psychology of Terrorism," http://essays.ssrc.org/sept11/essays/mccauley.htm.

Psychological Model of Terrorism

The psychologically-based model of terrorist studies posits that the causes of terrorism can be located in the individual terrorist's mind. This idea has been a major influence on the study of terrorism since the field's inception in the 1970s. These models assume that subconscious or pathological forces compel individuals to engage in terrorist activity. Within this school of thought, terrorists are commonly figured psychologically deviant or defective. Scholars have looked, among other things, to borderline personality disorder, anger issues, narcissism, and megalomania for explanations of why terrorism occurs, and why certain individuals participate in it.

What it does...

The psychology-based model may provide insight into the commitments, beliefs and actions of specific individuals who happen to be psychologically defective. As such, it may be important as a tool for understanding the actions of those specific individuals.

What it does not do...

The psychology-based model does not offer insight into, or provide a map of, general patterns of terrorist behavior, or even the behavior of groups. No evidence has been found to suggest that those who engage in terrorism in general suffer from psychological illnesses to any greater or lesser extent than other populations.

To think on:

Emphatic and often rabid attempts to reduce terrorists to a defective type of personality do little to assist the analyst and create impediments to understanding methods for disrupting, co-opting or removing essential issues related to terrorism.

Since mental defect is considered a mitigating circumstance within the legal system, doesn't the assumption that terrorists are "crazy" undermine their responsibility for their own criminal actions?

such horrific actions against non-combatants. Additionally, it looks simple: if the core cause of terrorism is an individual psychological defect, then the analyst has no need to examine the social, political, economic, cultural, and other levels of context. The issue of individual and group psychology is important, but not on the individual level. Social psychology then provides a way to contextualize the individual and his motivations within the social and political environment in which he operates. Students and analysts should therefore pay particular attention to the revised social-psychological models of terrorism by commentators such as Clark McCauley, John Horgan, Maxwell Taylor, and Fathali Moghaddam,[17] whose research is finally being given long-deserved acknowledgment in the field. This new, adapted model provides analysts with a much more solid base upon which to begin their research on the psychological forces at play in terrorism.

Cold War frames

Another dominant interpretative model within terrorism studies views terrorism as an expression of power political instrumentalism, known variously as "rational choice," "rational actor," or "strategic choice theory." This model recognizes and emphasizes an agent's power concerns and is closely related to the realist school of thought within international relations.[18] Within this model, groups' activities are understood in terms of reasoned and rational power struggles aimed at redressing

---

17 For instance see, Fathali M. Maghaddam, *From the Terrorist' Point of View: What They Experience and Why They Come to Destroy*, (Westport, Connecticut: Praeger Security International, 2006); John Horgan, "The search for the terrorist personality" in A. Silke (Ed.), *Terrorists, Victims, and Society: Psychological Perspectives on Terrorism and its Consequences* (England: John Wiley & Sons, 2003), pp.3-27; Maxwell Taylor, *The Terrorist* (London: Brassy's, 1988); Clark McCauley, *The Psychology of Terrorism*, http://essays.ssrc.org/sept11/essays/mccauley.htm.

18 For a concise explanation of political realism see, Hans J. Morgenthau, *Politics Among Nations: The Struggle for Power and Peace* (London: McGraw-Hill, 1993), pp. Martha Crenshaw, *Terrorism, Legitimacy, and Power* (Middletown, CT: Wesleyan University Press, 1982); 'An Organizational Approach to the Analysis of Political Terrorism,' in *Orbis*, vol. 29, no. 3, 1985, pp. 465-89; 'The Logic of Terrorism: Terrorist Behavior as a Product of Strategic Choice,' in Reich (op. cit.), pp. 7-24. 4-16.

"Rational Choice/Actor Model"

Rational choice models applied to terrorism assume that terrorist acts flow from rational decision making and that they are based on careful deliberation and the conscious calculation of costs and benefits, not pathological, subconscious urges or irrational passions. These rational decisions are instead elements of an optimal strategy—one that pursues real sociopolitical goals.

What it does...

Rational choice models give us a framework for analyzing the relationship between actions and objectives, causes and effects. In order to devise functional counter-terrorism efforts, we must know something about the thought processes behind terrorist actions. This model may be applied to weigh the utility of various policies and counter-measures. According to rational choice model, terrorists are discouraged from action when its cost is too high; in other words, they make a rational choice about what action to take and under which circumstances to take it. This is not a one-size-fits-all model: we still need to know the threshold level for each individual group.

What it does not do...

Rational choice is not a description of the everyday reality of terrorist groups, but a model that focuses on one aspect of decision-making processes. Rational calculation alone does not explain terrorism, nor does it override non-rational factors such as the pressures of clandestinity, desire for revenge, etc. Additionally, rationality must always be placed within social, political, and cultural contexts.

To think on:

The choices violent sub-state organizations make are rational from the ingroup perspective, but the analyst must resist seeing them as "mini-states." Organizations operating in a clandestine and resource constrained environment may well display different actions that are internally coherent, yet different from a State.

Is it realistic to assume that subnational, clandestine, tightly knit violent groups with scarce resources engage in cost/benefit analysis and match means to ends based on the same assumptions as a sovereign state acting on the global arena?

grievances and refashioning power structures in their favor. From this perspective, the terrorist or insurgent group is a unified and cohesive actor (very much like a state in the international arena) that through careful cost/benefit analysis, decides to use the terrorist "instrument" in its calculated pursuit of social dominance. This understanding of terrorism as a rational instrument underlies—either explicitly or implicitly—many of the major works on terrorism, notably Martha Crenshaw, who suggests that terrorism, "can be considered a reasonable way of pursuing extreme interests in the political arena."[19]

Terrorism as an academic field of inquiry came into being when the Cold War was raging and strategic choice theorizing reigned supreme among analysts of international politics. This framework's popularity is understandable, then; however, sub-state clandestine groups simply do not behave like state governments. Controlling territory, levying taxes, access to international

> **Clandestine:** characterized, done in, or executed with secrecy or concealment especially for purposes of subversion or deception
> (dictionary.com)

forums, the ability to employ coercive measures like the draft,—these (and many more) are the tools of the rational sovereign state. A terrorist group typically possesses none of these. That is not to say that terrorists are not rational, or that they do not use the means available to them after careful cost/benefit analysis. The dynamic, however, is different: states are sovereign entities while terrorist groups are clandestine substate entities. States levy taxes and raise armies, while terrorists groups engage in illegal action in order to raise funds and purchase arms on the black market. The heads of states rely on the rule of law, while terrorists run from the law. Though these are simplified dichotomies, they nevertheless show that the

---

19 Martha Crenshaw, *Terrorism, Legitimacy, and Power* (Middletown, CT: Wesleyan University Press, 1982); "An Organizational Approach to the Analysis of Political Terrorism," Orbis, Vol. 29, No. 3, (1985), pp. 465-89; "The Logic of Terrorism: Terrorist Behavior as a Product of Strategic Choice," in Walter Reich (ed.), *Origins of Terrorism: Psychologies, Ideologies, Theologies, States of Mind* (New York et alibi: Cambridge University Press, 1990), pp. 7-24.

Organizational Model

The organizational model considers terrorism a function of the internal structures and dynamics of the terrorist group itself. It assumes that a terrorist group's priority is organizational survival, over and above ideological principles and even the attainment of stated objectives. After all, if a group ceases to exist entirely, there is no chance of achieving any of its goals; as long as the group exists, there is some chance of achieving at least some of its goals.

What it does...

This model provides a partial insight into how terrorist groups, like many or perhaps even most organizations, become inwardly-focused and driven primarily by self-preservation. It is framework for thinking about the various ways in which the group itself may be important to the terrorist struggle.

What it does not do...

The organizational model does not describe all terrorist groups at all times, and it always requires some additional political, social and cultural context to make it truly useful. Depending on context, organizational requirements may cause a group to moderate its positions and tactics in order to ensure its survival. Conversely, it may cause the group to radicalize and escalate their tactics. It also may prompt a group to shift its political objectives in order to avoid fulfilling its stated aim, or it may compel them to take a hard line and change nothing.

To think on:

Groups take on organizational dynamics, but transnational drug cartels, insurgencies, gangs and terrorist groups are more fully understood by recognizing the four analytical markers of patron/client relationships, challenge/response cycle, limited good (resources) and the honor shame paradigm to which they are bound.

If we recognize that commitment to the existence of a charitable fraternity does not impose the same ethical, political, or practical demands as commitment to the existence of a terrorist group or an outlaw motorcycle club—how can the analyst explain those differences?

rules and prerogatives of statehood are typically not available to terrorists.

Scholars employing these frameworks—psychological, instrumental, organizational, and rational actor models—have made very useful contributions to the study of terrorism and terrorist groups. Their work offers partial and complementary insights into terrorism, but each is unable to provide an adequate framework for analysis on its own. This is not a complaint; rather, it is an observation. No analytical model alone is able to account for all aspects of terrorism. In our research on sub-state violent groups, we find that there are always multiple factors—social, ideological, theological, and others—framing rational choice, and an awareness of these many dynamics allows us to contextualize the instrumentality of violence and give a social setting for the psychology of individuals within groups. These larger background factors can be thought of as "frame the frames." The ways in which they overlap or differ allow us to understand why a group may choose one type of attack over another, why it may choose to escalate or moderate its tactics, what it considers an acceptable cost, why and how it seeks to achieve a particular objective, and so forth.

These larger frames need to be taken into consideration if analysis is to be accurate. It is clear that political and (perhaps especially) religious terrorist groups' actions are rarely rational in the very specific, goal-oriented Weberian sense that rational actor models demand (religious terrorism is explored further in chapter five).[20] While sub-state activist groups may not conform to the sort of rationality that tends to inform the actions of state governments, terrorist groups of all types nevertheless possess an internally coherent rationality.[21] To understand how this works, and how it works differently from case to case and from place to place, we need first to look at those larger frames in order to establish what is and is not

20 See Max Weber (trans. H. P. Secher), *Basic Concepts in Sociology* (London: Peter Owen, 1962), pp. 59-62.

21 Mark Jeurgensmeyer, *Terror in the Mind of God: The Global Rise of Religious Violence* (Berkley: University of California Press, 2000), pp. 119-243.

Instrumental Model

The instrumental model regards terrorism as an effort to achieve a certain set of objectives—the opposite of the self-perpetuating organizational approach. It assumes that terrorists are rational and that they use the threat or use of violence as a chip in the bargaining process of politics.

What it does...

The instrumental model offers a partial insight into terrorist decision making, providing a framework for thinking about how terrorists may match means and ends. Because terrorism is understood as an instrument of rational and optimized political change, groups are understood to be amenable to negotiation and settlement. This model therefore allows us to consider the possibility of breaking cycles of violence through political means.

What it does not do...

Like some of the previous models, it does not describe all terrorist groups all of the time, and like its counterpoint, the organizational model, it is always in need of additional political, social and cultural context. Depending on context, instrumental requirements may propel a group to moderate its positions and tactics in order reach an optimal settlement, or it may cause it to radicalize and escalate because accommodation seems unlikely.

To think on:

If the analyst has fully understood the context surrounding the groups' actions, relationships to other groups, people they claim to represent, governments and the historical and social contexts the instrumental model can be useful in conveying complex reasons to those seeking analysis. Absent the full contextual understanding the explanations become one-dimensional and may well lead to dangerous assumptions.

Even if groups are partially explained with reference to the objectives they pursue, can the analyst really explain the significance and implications of those objectives without also knowing something about the group and its context?

considered rational in the social, political, and theological context of the specific group we are examining. Contextual frames supply the rational choice model with a bounded rationality for the choices being made. They supply information on behavior that may seem psychologically deviant without the appropriate context, and they endow organizations with meaning and purpose. Contextual frames are nothing short of crucial to analysis.

It would be much easier for the analyst if the various groups comprising the terrorist universe could be explained by a single model or theory. Unfortunately, that is not the world in which we live. Individual tools then help us unpack the terrorism's various aspects and create typologies of terrorist groups, but they are ultimately only helpful when used in moderation, and not to the exclusion of others. They work best, in other words, when they overlap within a rigorous, replicable and defensible analytical framework. Throughout the rest of this book, we will argue that such a framework can be found in the social-psychological approach known as Social Identity Theory (SIT).[22]

---

22 For an early explanation of this approach, see David W. Brannan, Philip F. Esler, and N. T. Anders Strindberg, "Talking to 'Terrorists'".

Chapter Summary:

- Those engaged in terrorism studies have used a range of different frameworks, but it is fundamentally important that researchers use a rigorous theoretical scaffolding for their own work in order to more fully understand the causes, motivations and contexts of the group or phenomenon they are studying.

- In general, terrorism studies have been historically limited by relying too heavily on flawed or only partially effective models.

- The psychological model of terrorism studies has generally assumed that terrorists fall into a psychopathological profile on an individual level. This has been proven untrue, but more current social psychological approaches that provide explanations for behaviors of individuals within contextualized social and political environments are extremely useful when thinking about dynamics within terrorist groups.

- The rational choice model that emerged during the Cold War ascribes the qualities and modes of behavior of national entities to terrorist and other substate violent groups, making it difficult to account for the idiosyncratic ways in which terrorist groups are forced to operate, and the unique set of circumstances to which they must adapt.

- The organizational model views a terrorist group as an entity interested chiefly in preserving the organization itself, but it requires other theoretical modes in order to be truly useful in explaining terrorist behavior.

- The instrumental model sees terrorism as stemming from a rational decision to use violence as a bargaining chip in the political sphere in order to achieve a specific goal or set of goals. Like the organizational model, it requires pairing with another, more contextually-based theory, inn order to be really useful.

- The best theoretical frameworks are those that synthesize different approaches to analyzing terrorist groups and phenomena because they can account for a broader scope of context.

- Social Identity Theory (SIT), which will be introduced in following chapters, provides a broader, more flexible, and more effective way of looking at the behavior of terrorists on both the individual and group levels.

Thinking About Terrorism

3

Terrorism: A Sociological Perspective

Overview

Having examined the strengths, weaknesses, and potential pitfalls of the main models and frameworks used in the field of terrorism studies to date, we propose Social Identity Theory (SIT) as an effective framework for cross and multi-cultural analysis of sub-national violent groups. The use of SIT and the call for understanding context in analyses of terrorism and terrorists are sometimes confused with a view of such activities and actors as moral or otherwise acceptable. The framework does not require the analyst to either approve or condemn anything—it is not a moral, but an analytical framework. As such, however, it does demand that the researcher "understand" terrorist groups and their actions in a way that properly positions the analyst to achieve greater critical and analytical clarity.

Focus Questions:

- Why is a sociological perspective so important in terrorism studies?

- What does an SIT framework offer to the analyst that other popular models and theories preclude?

- Why does Betts argue that empathy for terrorist groups is critical to understanding them?

- How do group identities affect an individual's identity?

- What can happen when terrorist groups fail to provide their constituents with a positive social identity?

A number of renowned scholars have contributed their perspectives to how we should think about terrorism.[1] Martha Crenshaw, a leading voice in the terrorism studies community, has noted that groups' use of terrorist tactics is a strategic choice by rational actors.[2] Mark Juergensmeyer has described the tactical use of terrorist violence in an effort to change the political or social situation as "grand theater" in which terrorists plays out their vision of a cosmic war.[3] Noted religious terrorism scholar David Rapoport has explained the various "waves" of modern terrorism by comparing the behaviors and objectives of terrorist groups in the modern age with those of groups that operated as early as two thousand years ago.[4] Bruce Hoffman, long time RAND counter-terrorism specialist and Georgetown University professor, explains that the reason why terrorism

terrorism: the word terrorism as used in this book is imperfectly defined, recognized to be politically charged, is highly subjective, and is used to label our enemies, but is generally comprised of four essential elements:

- The threat or use of force
- with the intent to influence political or social situations,
- by affecting an audience beyond those directly targeted by the violence,
- and targeting those traditionally perceived as non-combatants in an effort to create fear.

---

1   Earlier and enduring efforts by Paul Wilkinson, Ted Gurr, Walter Laqueur and Brian Jenkins, among others, have defined the field and contributed to how we think about terrorism.
2   See for instance, Martha Crenshaw, "The logic of terrorism: Terrorist behavior as a product of strategic choice" in Walter Reich (ed), *Origins of Terrorism*, pp. 7-24.
3   Mark Juergensmeyer, *Terror in the Mind of God*, pp. 145-163; specifically as it relates to religious violence. Reza Aslan backs up Juergensmeyer's position with a sociological argument on how to defend against this type of attack in his work, *How to Win a Cosmic War: God Globalization, and the End of The War on Terror*, (New York: Random House, 2009).
4   David C. Rapoport, "Modern Terror: History and Special Features," in Andrew T. H. Tan, *The Politics of Terrorism: A Survey* (ed.) (London: Routledge, 2006) pp. 3-16.

is difficult to define is that the meaning of the word has changed over time,[5] and it is difficult to distinguish terrorism from other types of violence carried out by sub-national groups during insurgencies and guerrilla warfare. Nevertheless, a universal feature of terrorist groups is their focus on changing the socio-political status quo.[6]

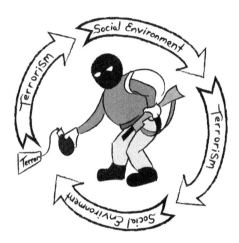

Throughout the literature and across its various models and approaches, there is an integral connection between the behavior and objectives of terrorist groups and the norms, pressures, and structures of the societies in which they operate.[7] Prussian military strategist Carl von Clausewitz (1780-1831), in his seminal work On War, argued that war is primarily a social endeavor, "the continuation of politics by other means."[8] The same can be said about terrorism. Anyone producing or consuming analysis on terrorism must take this insight seriously because it is the key to analysis: terrorism, always and everywhere, must be considered in context.[9] In terrorist conflicts, for both the attackers and those attacked, violence takes place in a social milieu of continuous feedback.[10] Terrorists

5   Bruce Hoffman, *Inside Terrorism* (New York: Columbia University Press, 2006), pp. 20-34.

6   Ibid., pp. 35-41.

7   This approach has been argued convincingly by Seth J. Schwartz, Curtis S. Dunkel, and Alan S. Waterman, "Terrorism: An Identity Theory Perspective," *Studies in Conflict and Terrorism*, Vol. 32, No. 6, June 2009, pp. 537-559. This is not to suggest that all commentators acknowledge the relationship.

8   Carl von Clausewitz, *On War*, (ed. and trans.) Michael Howard and Peter Paret; (Princeton: Princeton University Press, 1976).

9   For an earlier related argument on the subject, see, David W. Brannan, Philip F. Esler and N.T. Anders Strindberg, "Talking to Terrorists, pp. 3-24.

10 For an excellent general discussion of these issues, see Clark McCauley's "Psychological Issues in Understanding Terrorism and the Response to Terrorism," in Bruce Bongar, et. al.,(Eds.), *Psychology of Terrorism,* (Oxford: Oxford University Press, 2007), pp. 13-31.

are impacted by their social environment, and their violence in turn impacts the social environment. Tactics, targeting, the level of violence, willingness to negotiate, support structures, political agendas, and strategic objectives—these are all framed by the social realities within which terrorists exist. This demonstrates how truly complex terrorism is as a political phenomenon, but it does not create an insurmountable barrier to analysts. In fact, it gives the analyst multiple data points as he or she constructs an analysis of what has been called "propaganda by deed."[11]

Terrorism is a form of social interaction. While some forms of social interaction are almost universally recognizable, many can only really be properly understood within a relevant social and cultural context.[12] Embedding SIT in particular cultural settings powerfully illuminates the capacity of the Emic—that is, the indigenous, or native point of view—in dialogue with the Etic—the informed outsider, or the social scientific point of view.

> **Emic:** a description of behavior or a belief in terms meaningful (consciously or unconsciously) to the actor; that is, an emic account comes from a person within the culture
> *(princeton.edu)*

> **Etic:** a description of a behavior or belief by an external observer, in terms that can be applied to other cultures
> *(princeton.edu)*

Why Social Identity Theory?

In short, SIT argues that a group's behavior and relationships to other groups can be accounted for by examining both its social context and its members'

---

11 A term made famous by a small Russian group, which challenged the Czar during the 1870-80s. See Bruce Hoffman, *Inside Terrorism* pp. 4-9 for an excellent review of the development of the term and how it influenced the development of terror groups.

12 For an earlier related argument on the subject, see, David W. Brannan, Philip F. Esler and N.T. Anders Strindberg, "Talking to Terrorists, pp. 3-24.

Social Movement Model

The social movement model states that terrorist groups are elements and products of wider social movements that have broken off from the mainstream and turned to violence. The group typically splits from the mainstream due to some combination of ideological conviction, tactical preference, and the need to mobilize resources.

What it does...

This model provides insight into how some terrorist groups may connect to a context much wider than its own core supporters, forcing analysts to take into account the importance of a group's broader sociopolitical context.

What it does not do...

It does not, however, describe all terrorist groups all of the time. Since it tends to view terrorist groups as a fringe of something larger—a malfunction within some social movement—it tends to reduce terrorists to futile extremists, destined to be bypassed by history. This does not adequately account for the numerous terrorist organizations that have created social movements and even gone on to form governments. Additionally, the model requires group specific historical and cultural context.

To think on:

If the Social Movement Model alone was singularly capable of providing an analytical framework for understanding terrorism, why are there multiple, competing and enduring groups that represent social movements?

For instance, the various Palestinian organizations that represent—and fail to represent—the Palestinian people are often at odds with each other and much greater contextual understanding is needed to effectively analyze the situation effectively than merely understanding the groups to be splinters from the larger movement.

understanding of themselves and their group within that context. That is to say, SIT posits the Emic as the critical starting point for the investigative project. Rather than forcing the subject into externally-constructed and ill-fitting frameworks devised by researchers (the Etic view), sometimes independent of the specific reality of the group, SIT is attentive not only to context, but also to the ways in which that context is viewed and acted upon by the group. In this way, SIT offers a framework for integrating insights from a variety of analytical models within an intercultural framework, including the ones discussed in the previous chapter.[13] Importantly, it also allows the researcher to account for his or her own hermeneutic biases, as well as those of the research subject. By using a sociological framework such as SIT for analysis, a researcher can account for a

hermeneutic: a method or principle of interpretation
(Merriam-Webster.com)

variety of important contexts impacting the world views, actions, and agendas of terrorist groups and individuals. Culture, ideology, and religion impact the "how" and "why" of terror groups. Using SIT as a framework, analysts can view terrorist conflict as a product of collective life rather than effects of individual pathology.[14]

As Moghaddam explains, "A major reason for the considerable international influence of social identity theory is that the theory leaves room for cultural variations but at the same time presents substantial and specific postulates."[15] This capability—general applicability and specific insights—makes

---

13 Early and important work on SIT include, Henry Tajfel and J.C. Turner, "An Integrative theory of intergroup conflict" in, W. G. Austin and S. Worchel (Eds), *The Social Psychology of Intergroup Relations,* (Monterey, CA: Brooks/Cole, 1979), pp. 33-47. For a succinct and insightful explanation of SIT as it relates to the topic at hand, see, Fathali M. Moghaddam, *Multiculturalism and Intergroup Relations: Psychological Implications for Democracy in Global Context,* (Washington, DC: American Psychological Association, 2008), pp. 92-99. For a description of how this analytical framework has been used in relation to Islamic terrorism specifically, see Fathali M. Moghaddam, *How Globalization Spurs Terrorism: The Lopsided Benefits of "One World" and Why That Fuels Violence,* (Westport, CT: Praeger Security International, 2008) pp. 10-35.

14 Ibid, Moghaddam, *Multiculturalism and Intergroup Relations,* p. 93.

15 Ibid, Moghaddam, p. 94.

Culture

Culture is understood as the different ways in which humans structure and organize their social affairs. Among many other things, these structures give rise to different sets of behaviors and expectations—different norms for how people are expected to interact with each other. Cultural frameworks affect what and how people say and do. Cultures are complex, dynamic and overlapping.

What it does...

Culture provides a map of general patterns of behavior that can be assumed to influence, but not define, terrorist behavior. This includes how terrorists expect their actions to be received by the ingroup, the wider constituency, and various outgroups. These patterns are cultural stereotypes, models of reality, that help us trace main ideas, assumptions, norms, and cues.

What it does not do...

Because cultures are not static but change over time, and because all individuals and groups are influenced by other factors as well as culture, culture alone does not explain "why they do it" any more than it could explain why the analyst engages in analysis. Also, when simple models are confused with nuanced reality, analysts are invariably led to flawed conclusions.

To think on:

If the influence of "Christian culture" is different in Southern Alabama and rural Greece, why would we assume that the influence of "Islamic culture" is the same in all Islamist groups regardless of where they emerge?

SIT valuable even beyond the analytical task. It can also serve as a basis for practitioners engaging in counter-terrorism and conflict resolution. SIT helps analysts untangle the dynamic relationships between individuals and their groups. It shows when and how those groups are changing, when they will be impacted by opportunities for interaction or interdiction, and how groups' constantly-negotiated, socially-constructed identity might allow a group to migrate from terrorism to non-violent political activity. In short, SIT is valuable at almost every level of the effort to understand, manage, and counter terrorism.

Understanding terrorists?

Terrorist groups are just that—groups of people. As such they can be analyzed and explained, and their motives and goals can be understood (and thus defended against) by using tools like SIT that give analysts a broader conception of how they work.[16]

To understand something in an analytical sense is not the same as "understanding" in the sense of justifying or excusing behaviors. As Columbia University professor Richard Betts suggests:

> Understanding radical groups in other cultures is difficult. Insight requires a degree of empathy, and parochial observers find it hard to empathize with different worldviews, while cosmopolitan observers naturally find reactionary ideologies alien and unfathomable. It is also vital to distinguish between empathy and sympathy. Anyone who appears to sympathize with terrorists will be discredited as a source of wisdom on counterterrorism, but those who do not empathize with

---

16 For a very accessible discussion which gives a "how to" approach for those researching social movements, see, Donatella Della Porta and Mario Diani, *Social Movements: An Introduction* (Oxford: Blackwell, 2000), especially pp. 83-109, for a discussion of the relationship between the ongoing negotiation of identity and collective action.

terrorists will not get far enough inside their heads to develop the maximum base of intelligence for counterterrorism.

Betts continues:

> This does not mean that we should meet terrorist demands, but rather that knowing the enemy better increases the odds of finding an opening in his armor, or of figuring out better ways to use propaganda (what "public diplomacy" for the war on terror really means) to sway the populations whose allegiance is at issue.[17]

Betts makes a convincing argument for why responsible analysts should seek to understand groups that operate according to much different cultural, political, or moral compasses than one's own. Like Betts we don't want the reader to sympathize with terrorists

empathy: the experience of understanding another person's condition from their perspective.
(Psychologytoday.com)

but terrorism analysts must take the sociological nuance seriously. These realities may often seem distant from enforcement, military, or intelligence concerns; things like social structures, theological convictions, and cultural codes may not appear immediately relevant to counter-terrorism. Yet the limited utility of models discussed in the previous chapter is directly correlated to the failure to take such surrounding factors seriously. If we can dare to see terrorism as part of a broader picture provided by sociological research, we will find even more insight into the "dynamic, amorphous and constantly evolving" nature of terrorism.[18]

---

17 Richard Betts, *Analysis, War, and Decision*, p. 4.
18 Terms consistently used by Bruce Hoffman in conversation with one of the authors (DWB) between 1996 to 2004 to describe the phenomenon of terrorism.

Why does anyone belong to a group?

For our purposes, a group can be defined as any given body of people who think of themselves as a distinct group. It may be very small (e.g. the Abu Nidal Organization) or very large (e.g. the United States); it may be an

> **group:** some number of people (from very few to very many) who are united around a common interest, purpose, or practice, and who think of themselves as connected in some way.

organization, such a terrorist group, or a larger and more abstract "framework," such as a religion or a culture with which one identifies. When individuals come together and engage with each other in a group setting, the group becomes a source of their socially constructed identity. At the same time, the individual contributes (to a greater or lesser degree depending on the size and nature of the group) to the identity of the group.

The experience of belonging to a group determines the identities of most individuals in a powerful way. When we join or leave groups that are important to us, we redefine who we are. Because our group memberships become parts of our identity, any value associated with those groups will have implications for our feelings of self-worth. Examples of this might be taking pride in achievements of one's corps, or feeling shame for a crime committed by a colleague.[19] To understand how this works, it is helpful to look to Henri Tajfel, the originator of SIT, who identified three components of what it means for the individual to belong to a group.

---

19 Rupert Brown, *Group Processes: Dynamics Within and Between Groups* (Oxford: Basil Blackwell, 1988), pp. 20-22.

Identity

Identity is the perception an individual has of what makes himself, himself--his assumed self-image. This involves the capacity for self-reflection, knowing who you are, and how you relate to other individuals and groups. Identity is a powerful motivator--who you believe you are will impact what you believe you should or need to do. It is also important to note that identity is not constant, but constantly developing. In other words, who we believed we were in high school is not the same as who we believe we are thirty years later.

Identities are also ascribed, or assigned, by others. Terrorist analysts analyze terrorism, and in the process tend to ascribe a "terrorist identity" to their subjects. The subjects themselves, however, think of themselves as warriors, freedom fighters, revolutionaries, or in some other (likely more flattering) role. This is an example of dissonance between assumed and ascribed identities.

Most importantly ....

Because identity is a powerful force, we have to prioritize assumed identity over the ascribed identity. Terrorists' beliefs about who they are will help us understand the things they say and do.

To think on:

If you were a British subject at the time of the American Revolution, would you have perceived attacks by the Sons of Liberty against other British subjects as terrorism?

1. **a cognitive component,** the knowledge that one belongs to a group.

2. **an evaluative component,** the positive or negative connotation of the group and of one's membership of it.

3. **an emotional component,** the emotions that accompany the cognitive and evaluative components, such as pride in and love of one's own group, hatred, fear, respect, etc. towards other groups.[20]

According to Tajfel, social identity may be defined as that part of an individual's self-concept that is derived from these three components, regardless of the specific size, structure, or scope of the group, whether the group is the FBI, the Knights of Columbus, the Aryan Nations, or Islam. As illustrated here, groups can range from small organizations to broad national or religious collectives. What matters is that we not only know that we are members, but that we attach values and emotions to our membership.[21]

---

20 Henri Tajfel, *Differentiation between Social Groups: Studies in the Social Relations of Intergroup Relations* (London et alibi: Academic Press, 1978), p. 28.

21 Henri Tajfel, "La catégorisation sociale" in S. Moscovici (ed.) *Introduction à la Psychologie Sociale*, Vol. 1 (Paris: Larousse, 1972), p. 31.

Identities are complex, but they also overlap. That is to say, while each source of identity has three components, each individual also has several sources of identity. The best way to describe this dynamic is by using a concrete example. A member of Hizbullah might think of himself as Lebanese, as a farmer, as belonging to the lower class, as Shi'a, as Muslim, as Arab, as a member of Hizbullah, as a member of Hizbullah's military wing, as a non-commissioned officer, as an artillerist, and so forth. All of these identifications derive from group memberships, and each has the power to generate and guide action. In addition, he might identify with a particular mosque, he might be a member of a literary society, a stamp collectors' society, and the Lebanese PTA. An individual is made up of a multiplicity of identities that are tied to a full range of human interests, inclinations, and life goals.

Overlapping identities often result in tensions that an individual must resolve. A Hizbullah militant, for instance, has a Muslim identity that may propel him towards a sense of solidarity with other Muslim fighters in the region, but he also has a Lebanese nationalist identity, which incentivizes his domestic political focus. Additionally, he has a Shi'a identity that generates some affinity towards Iran, but that also balances against the local focus inherent in his Lebanese identity. Hizbullah, in particular, relies on its members and sympathizers identifying themselves primarily as Lebanese Shi'a. Its ideological agenda is a reflection of this membership profile, which means that it contains an inherent tension between a regional and a local focus. Hizbullah members and supporters expect the group to enhance their social status—to add positive value and emotion to their lives—which means that the group needs to retain both its regional focus and importance, as well as its domestic practical political focus. This is a tension that most Western analysts seem unwilling or unable to take seriously when they characterize Hizbullah as merely an Iranian proxy, the extended arm of Tehran on Israel's borders.

"Ingroup/Outgroup Dynamic"

A person's ingroup is the group to which he/she belongs, and an outgroup is any and all other groups. A person usually has several ingroup identifications (e.g. American, Lutheran, New Yorker, police officer, SWAT-team member). In order to remain relevant and viable, ingroups provide members with positive ingroup identities. In part, this is done in competition with outgroups for resources, membership, legitimacy, etc.

Due to this very particular constellation of identities, Hizbullah has virtually no non-Shi'a or non-Lebanese members (even though its support base extends far outside both those groups). Because the membership in the organization does not add positive value to those who are not bound to that very particular community, it does not make sense in terms of value for a non-Lebanese or a non-Shi'a person to join it. If a group fails to add positive value to an individual's sense of who he or she is, there is no reason to join or remain a member or supporter. One caveat to this statement: state support, or patronage, does not follow this rule. We will deal with this particular kind of relationship later in the book. For now what we need to keep in mind is that without loyal and enthusiastic members, any group lacks viability.

To understand what motivates someone to become and remain a member of any particular group, we first have to understand his or her dominant sources of social identification, and how they compare in status and strength with other competing sources of social identification.[22] This process requires us to research, analyze, understand, and explain several layers of complex social and cultural realities, each of which will be different for individual members. However, when we study groups rather than individuals, it is not only permissible, but necessary

---

22 Michael A. Hogg and Dominic Abrams, *Social Identifications: A Social Psychology of Intergroup Relations and Group Processes* (London and New York: Routledge, 1988), pp. 12-16.

to generalize based on what we understand as the social identity issues of the "average" or "aggregate" membership and leadership of the group.

The single most important premise of SIT is this: to understand the complexity of terrorist groups and movements, we have to reject the notion that there is a single issue (i.e. mental illness, a "global terrorist ideology", hatred of freedom) that can be applied to any and all terrorists. Instead, we have to understand terrorists as individuals and terrorist groups as groups of individuals that are driven—at the most basic level—by the same mechanisms, wants, and needs as non-terrorists. Because of the complex nature of this type of analysis, SIT necessarily forces the researcher to specialize, or to acquire a deeper knowledge of a smaller number of groups. This makes it more difficult than single-cause, one-size-fits-all explanations, but also far more useful, as we demonstrate throughout this book. It is a useful tool for any analyst, not just the "terrorist expert."

SIT and group conflict

What makes SIT particularly important to the study of terrorist groups and movements are its attendant models for understanding intergroup relations and conflict (schematically illustrated in "Intergroup Relations and Conflict" sketch at the end of this chapter). The previous section suggested that to the individual terrorist, the terrorist group is a source of social identity, and that this identity hinges on the positive value and positive emotional attachment of group membership. Within the terrorist group, as within all other groups, certain sets of norms and standards define the views, beliefs, and behaviors that are considered acceptable for group members, thus establishing, maintaining, and enhancing group identity.[23] These norms, and the politicization of these norms, are supplied by group elites.[24]

---

23 Rupert Brown, *Group Processes*, pp. 42-48.
24 Hugh Seton-Watson, *Nations and States* (London: Methuen, 1977), p. 10.

Against this background, SIT suggests that groups have a fundamental need to provide their members with a positive social identity—to establish a positively valued distinctiveness from other groups—in order to maintain their existence. When the identities and associated political interests of one group clash with those of another group, the result can be political conflict, including insurgency and terrorist violence. As we noted in the previous section, if the negative feelings that an individual member gets from belonging to a terrorist group outweigh the positive, this becomes an incentive for that individual to leave the group, which in turn weakens the group's cohesion and stability. This then is likely to negatively impact other members' assessments of their group membership, creating a downward spiral of disintegration.

Turning our focus on intergroup relations, if membership of, or attachment to another group (the "outgroup") with which the terrorist group competes is considered more positive than membership of one's own group ("ingroup"), this provides the individual with incentive to question or reevaluate the meaningfulness of ingroup membership in relationship to outgroup membership. On the individual level, this may serve as an incentive to defect—to cross over to the outgroup—which may lead to disintegration of the ingroup.

The ingroup is thus incentivized to retain its defecting members by redressing the whatever imbalance is causing its members dissatisfaction.

An example of this dynamic could be seen when the Popular Front for the Liberation of Palestine (PFLP) and the Democratic Front for the Liberation of Palestine (DFLP) competed for the Palestinian secular progressive constituency in the early 1970s. After the DFLP split off from the PFLP, the two locked into a pattern of fierce competition. Military capabilities and successes, charismatic leadership, and political clout through regional and international alignments made up the stock in trade of this rivalry. Each group sought to supply its members with a positive social identity through direct competition with, and at the direct expense of, the other. This competition has been integral to the ongoing development of the groups' distinct identities, even though the political programs of the PFLP and DFLP gradually became virtually identical (a similarity that also was an outcome of competition). In 2012, when one of the present authors asked a member of the DFLP leadership to identify the factor that prevented the two groups from merging, his answer was "almost nothing… except group identities."

Similar dynamics have taken place on the far right in the United States, in the context of competition between various Klan groups, Identity churches, and militia movements. A group's survival, and therefore the attainment of its ideological objectives, depends on its ability to supply members with a positively-valued social identity. In general, when a group's ability to make a positive contribution to its members' social identities is diminished, its viability becomes threatened. In such situations, two broad responses are open to group members discontented with their negatively charged social identities. One response is social mobility, which simply means that individual members leave the ingroup to join the outgroup. The feasibility of this option depends on the permeability of intergroup boundaries,[25] which are determined by external constraints (for

---

25 Michael A. Hogg and Dominic Abrams, *Social Identifications*, p. 54.

example, negative views or obstacles in the group to which access is sought), and internal constraints (disapproval and punishment of splitters within the ingroup).

Social mobility between terrorist groups tends to be rare due to the tightly knit and often highly secretive nature of these groups, as well as the group's disapproval and swift

> **social mobility:** the movement of individuals from ingroup to outgroup.
>
> **Not likely with terrorist groups**

punishment—strong deterrents that typically accompany actions understood as treasonous.

When social mobility is impossible or undesirable, the alternative response is social change, a pro-active collective effort to improve the positive values and emotional associations of ingroup members in relation to a dominant outgroup. This response is highly likely in the case of groups and organizations in which disapproval of dissidents is high and from

> **social change:** proactive collective effort by ingroup to improve its positive social identity in order to retain group members. Can be brought about through **social creativity** or **social competition**.
>
> ** Likely response in terrorist groups. **

which defection is difficult—characteristics of virtually all terrorist groups. Social change can be brought about through social creativity or social competition, or a combination of both.[26]

Social creativity involves an effort by the ingroup to redefine and manipulate the premises of their competition with a dominant outgroup. This is most common when the negative balance cannot be redressed in reality. This may involve redefining the value of some existing comparison, such as, for example, turning a weakness into strength ("our group may be small, but that allows us to be more nimble and stealthy"). This has been common among radical leftist

---

26 Philip F. Esler, *Galatians* (London: Routledge, 1998), p. 52.

groups that see themselves as the "vanguard of the revolution" or the "intellectual elite" that must educate the masses to join their fight against the world capitalist system.

Social creativity may also mean introducing the idea that true positive values are, by definition, the antithesis of those espoused by the outgroup (i.e. "our enemies are God's enemies and therefore are not only evil but destined for doom"). Examples include the European fascist movement, which, in the late 1980s believed that the secular fascist cause was futile. In order to avoid disintegration, several leading groups adopted a "spiritual perspective," making their enemies the enemies of God and thereby elevating the importance of the struggle, as well as equating defection with abandoning God's cause.

Finally, an ingroup may compare itself to some outgroup other than the dominant one, thereby bringing about a more favorable comparative situation (i.e. "white trash syndrome"—when impoverished whites in the South during Jim Crow lorded over African Americans in similar economic circumstances as a way of mitigating the humility of their own social and economic standing). Social creativity, then, is largely a matter of inculcating and indoctrinating group members with a new sense of themselves and their group's purpose. The practice shows clearly that what the outside world views as adverse in objective reality may be sidestepped by the group leadership in an attempt to enhance members' social identity and thus protect group cohesion. Our view of reality depends on what we need that reality to be and do for us—which is precisely why the emic, rather than the etic perspective needs to be the starting point for analysis.

Social creativity can be either a process of rationalizing adverse reality, or of sincere spiritual or ideological "enlightenment." Often the two blend together to the point that they become difficult to distinguish from each other. Social creativity may be understood as mental and emotional mechanisms that enable group members to cling to their cause in the face of "objective adversity." Entrenching oneself deeper in the righteousness of one's cause (making the cause more righteous and/or the enemy more evil), rather than admitting that what one has struggled and perhaps killed for has turned out to be wrong and pointless, is a very human response. Within terrorist groups, the group dynamic and its objectives often become inseparable from members' social identities. As group-think sets in, members re-evaluate adverse reality in ways that make their group memberships meaningful, sometimes in spite of reality. The fact that the dismantling of terrorist groups often produces violent splinters that not only increase the level of violence, but broaden the scope of targeting, relates directly to this process of social creativity.

Social competition, then, refers to the subordinate group's effort to improve its actual social status vis-à-vis a dominant group. This means taking on the outgroup within the framework of the ongoing struggle and intensifying, rather than redefining or circumventing, the competitive relationship. This effort brings with it direct intergroup conflict because "any threat to the distinctively superior position of a group implies a potential loss of positive comparisons and possible negative comparisons, which must be guarded against." That is to say, since each group's ability to supply its members with a positively-valued social identity determines its cohesion and viability relative to the other, each group will struggle against negative comparisons in order to maintain membership and avoid the downward spiral of disintegration. As noted above, without members there is no group, and without a group, there is no possibility of attaining whatever objectives the group pursues.

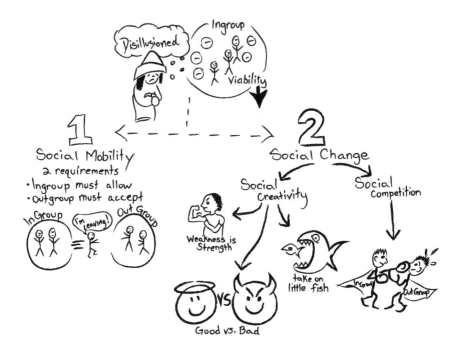

Intergroup Relations and Conflict

When a group member (or members) become disillusioned, some change must occur. Members will not stay in a group that is not providing them with a positive social identity, so change might happen in a couple of ways:

1. The member (or members) may leave the current ingroup and defect to the outgroup. This is called **Social Mobility** and can only happen if the ingroup allows them to leave and if they are accepted into the outgroup.

2. The alternative is **Social Change**, a collective effort by the ingroup to prevent defections by improving members' feelings about the group and its actions. This is done through either Social Creativity or Social Competition.

    *   Social Creativity occurs when a group chooses to redefine their goals or narrative to fit with the changes in context.

    *   Social Competition takes place when dominant groups compete directly for people or resources.

Terrorism: A Sociological Perspective

Chapter Summary:

- Terrorist groups and their behavior is best understood from within the social, political, religious, and global contexts in which they operate.

- The "Etic" describes the behavior or belief of a person/group as described by an outsider, while the "Emic" describes the way a behavior or belief is seen by the person/group from within.

- The social movement model regards terrorist groups as offshoots of larger, mainstream political groups, but it should be noted that not all terrorist groups lack some sort of larger cultural legitimacy.

- Culture is a social structure through which humans organize their thought and make sense of experience; as such, it provides a useful set of coordinates from which the analyst can begin to navigate his or her understanding of a group.

- Henri Tajfel gives us a helpful way of thinking about why people choose to belong to groups: because they provide members with a positive cognitive component, evaluative component, and emotional component.

- According to SIT, an individual's sense of self and self-worth is derived from the associations he or she has with the groups of which he or she is a part.

- Identity is determined at the individual level ("I think of myself as X"), but we can also ascribe identities to others ("I believe he or she is Y"). Although analysts ascribe identities to given individuals or groups, they should seriously consider the way that these individuals or groups "see" themselves.

- Identities are complex, varied, ever-changing, and sometimes contradictory. This complex layering affects the way an individual acts and perceives the world, and an effective analyst will attend to its various dynamics.

- Group members derive some kind of value from being a part of the group they are in; if this value becomes too negative, they will try to find a way out of the group (social mobility) or the group itself will have to change to make its members feel more positively about it (social change).

- If the group moves toward the social change model, they can achieve it by two different strategies: social competition or social creativity.

4

Analytical Markers

Overview

Groups operating in resource constrained environments, especially those under pressure for survival, exhibit a number of similar traits, or "markers." Sociological and anthropological research, particularly related to groups competing for resources in the Eastern Mediterranean region, has identified patterns of patron-client relationships, interactions centered on the acquisition of honor and avoidance of shame, perceptions of a "limited good," and behaviors of "challenge and response," as being central to group action and interaction. These scholarly insights, however, have a much more general applicability and can be used effectively within a Social Identity Theory framework to analyze most groups operating under similar circumstances. These four standard mechanisms whereby groups compete for resources and seek to ensure their own survival are difficult to pry apart. They feed into each other and make up a coherent whole, giving the analyst multiple points of reference in the effort to analyze group behavior.

Focus Questions:

- Why are the Mediterranean cultural markers (patron-client relationships, honor/shame paradigm, issues of limited good and the "challenge and response" model) useful to terrorism analysts?

- Why is public perception important when evaluating challenge and response interactions among terrorist groups?

- How are patron-client relationships mutually beneficial?

- How is one's honor affected by the idea of "limited good"?

There are four primary analytical traits or considerations—we refer to these as markers—in light of which the actions of terrorist groups can be considered: the patron-client relationship, the honor/shame paradigm, the challenge and response cycle, and the issue of "limited good" (which is about a limited resource, not an ethical evaluation). These markers are important when analyzing a terrorist group or a series of actions or attacks by terrorist groups, or when looking at threat issues related to terrorist groups, especially the possible relationship between known groups.[1] The use of these markers does not give an analyst a deterministic matrix of all possible actions—"if X therefore Y"—but rather offers a fluid matrix within which terrorist groups and their actions can be explored by systematically unpacking events and relationships. The goal is to get beyond the customary frames for understanding terrorist-related phenomena most commonly provided by media and public figures in order to uncover contextual relevance that offers a deeper insight into the realities of a given group, event, or alignment. This, in turn, enables more effective policy design and resource allocation, and a more accurate and comprehensive threat assessment.

For the sake of clarity, we will describe these analytical considerations as four separate markers; however, as groups act and respond to each other and their environment, the analyst must remember that these markers are dynamic and intimately interconnected. Nearly every action, exchange, or relationship of the terrorist group involves combinations of positive or negative honor challenges, both in relation to their patron-client relationships and to their perspective of the limited good for which they are contending. Put simply, these markers work in concert, and our ability to discern them will provide us with a greater understanding of situations, groups, and actions.

---

1   These markers are also evident in groups and organizations more generally, but their systematic application is most helpful when applied to violent and clandestine subnational organizations.

Foundational to this dynamic view of groups and movements is the challenge and response cycle, a model for understanding the processes whereby groups and individuals create and maintain (or challenge and disrupt) relations; this dynamic applies to patron-client relations as well as alignments and conflicts among equals. It originally grew out of a scholarly study of prevalent patterns of behavior in Eastern Mediterranean and Middle Eastern cultures. Among other things, anthropologist and sociologists found two factors in particular to be deeply ingrained and crucial for virtually all social interaction.[2] First, a strong identification of individuals with the groups to which they belong, as opposed to the individualistic assumptions that are prevalent in North America and Western Europe. Second, and a strong sense of individual and collective honor: the sense that virtually every instance of social interaction outside the immediate family is seen as a contest for honor.

Applying the markers to terrorist groups

More recent research has shown that similar traits are prevalent among members of terrorist groups, and that scholars can fruitfully transfer the challenge-response model from its original cultural context to the organizational terrorist context.[3] Here it is important to note the precise nature of the connection: it is not suggested that terrorism builds on or flows from Eastern Mediterranean cultures. It is suggested, however, that the traits and mechanisms that have developed over millennia in the Eastern Mediterranean for small group survival in a context of

---

2   For foundational literature, see, for instance, J. G. Peristiany (ed.) *Honour and Shame: The Values of Mediterranean Society* (London: Weidenfeld & Nicolson, 1965); David D. Gilmore (ed.), *Honour and Shame and the Unity of the Mediterranean* (Washington, DC: American Anthropological Association, 1987); Julian Pitt-Rivers (ed.), *Mediterranean Countrymen: Essays in the Social Anthropology of the Mediterranean* (Paris and La Haye: Mouton & Co, 1963).

3   David W. Brannan, Philip F. Esler and Anders Strindberg "Talking to Terrorists". Those markers are relevant to analysis of most sub-national groups in resource constrained environments. This includes terrorist groups, but also non-terrorist groups like outlaw motorcycle clubs and street gangs.

resource constraints are also discernible in small groups seeking to survive in other contexts of conflict and scarcity. That is to say, what anthropologists have found in the Eastern Mediterranean is an optimal model for small group survival; as such, it can be duplicated elsewhere and by other groups that may have no connection at all to that geographic area.

The central mechanism of the challenge-response cycle lies in public exchanges between individuals or groups whereby they establish their social rank or status. Since social status exists only through public perception and evaluation (see the challenge and response cycle chart), exchanges must be publicly visible. The contest for status between groups takes place through positive or negative honor challenges. Because they are socially evaluated, the precise nature of a challenge depends on its context. In general, however, positive challenges are those that establish or reinforce a positive relationship, such as a gift, a pledge of assistance, a statement of support, and so forth. Negative challenges are those that establish or reinforce a negative relationship, such as an armed attack, verbal abuse, or an alliance that challenges the interests of the other group.

> **honor challenge:** a claim to enter the social space of another that can be positive or negative.
> *(Malina, Bruce J., The New Testament world: Insights from Cultural Anthropology, p.34)*

Regardless of whether it is negative or positive, when a group makes an an honor challenge against another, it is publicly evaluated as either successful or unsuccessful. A successful negative challenge will enhance the social status of the challenger at the expense of the challenged, while a failed negative challenge may either have the opposite result, or simply reinforce the status quo. Similarly, a successful positive honor challenge will establish or enhance a positive relationship, either between equals (referred to as a "colleague contract") or two unequal parties in which one is a patron and the other a client. This is not a concept new to political thought; in fact, Aristotle identified this precise dynamic over two

Analytical Marker Cheat Sheet

The following cultural markers have proven highly relevant when analyzing clandestine terrorist organizations with a strong collective identity.

Patron-Client Relationship: A symbiotic relationship between groups or individuals in which the client relies on the patron for introductions, status, protection, or materials while the patron relies on the client to support, serve, and defend the patron.

Honor/Shame Paradigm: Honor is the publicly mediated and acknowledged positive status afforded to groups in relation to their friends and foes, while shame is the negatively charged opposite of honor.

Limited Good: A limited resource related to the honor of the group, which can be either a physical resource like land or an intangible resource like status.

Challenge/Response Cycle: The mode of interaction between competing groups in resource scarce environments.

 **For Instance ...**

...for those within the Palestinian national movement, a significant "limited good" issue is control over contested Palestinian/Israeli land. The honor of the Palestinian people is tied up in this limited resource, and is therefore an important touchstone for all Palestinian political, militant, and terrorist groups. Both positive and negative actions taken by the group can be understood in relation to the group's attempt to gain honor (which amounts to status or "social capital") in relation to that limited good (or resource).

- An attack on Israel is thus a negative honor challenge in relation to the limited good of the land.
- Praising the actions of an entity that recognizes Palestinian legitimacy is a positive honor challenge in relation to the limited good of the land.

thousand years ago: "Inferiors revolt in order that they may be equal and equals that they may be superior. Such is the state of mind that creates revolutions."[4]

Moving from more general principles to specifics, we can identify terrorism as a form of public communication whereby one group attempts to improve its standing vis-à-vis some other group. This "other group" is usually a government, but also can be a competing terrorist groups. Because it is a form of political public communication, terrorism only works if it can be perceived, assessed, and evaluated by a target audience (i.e. the public and/or policy makers). Indeed, terrorism hinges on the effort to make a "public proclamation" by damaging the credibility and status of its adversary through acts of violence. Thus, the challenge and response cycle is integral to terrorism.

Challenge ∘ ∘ ∘ ∘ ∘ ∘

---

4 Aristotle, Politics, VII.

Understanding the challenge and response cycle

The challenge and response model is a process comprised of three main components:

1. **Challenge:** some action or statement on the part of a group.
2. **Perception:** the perception of that action by the challenged group and by the public at large.
3. **Response:** the challenged group's reaction, immediately followed by an evaluation of that response by the public. Failure to respond is in itself a response that will be evaluated by the public.

Though it may at first seem shameful, an unsuccessful challenge may nevertheless win the hearts and minds of the public and be evaluated as "valiant" and "heroic," despite its failure. In this way, "failure" sometimes reinforces popular support and social status. Similarly, a non-response by the challenged group is not automatically seen as a failure, but may be evaluated as "the honorable thing to do" (for example, the decision not to bomb a terrorist facility located in a civilian residential area). The public nature of the challenge, the response, and evaluation of both is essential, and it is entirely shaped by the social, cultural, and political context of the specific conflict.

Terrorist targeting demonstrates this dynamic clearly and consistently. Aware that they are unable to succeed by "normal" military means, terrorist groups often use violence to embarrass and insult their enemy. They exploit weaknesses in order to provoke their enemy into overreacting—this overreaction could manifest itself as violent retaliation or extreme counter-measures. Thus, terrorist targets tend to be highly symbolic and/or vulnerable as part of an effort to "expose" the enemy's inability to defend itself and its people.

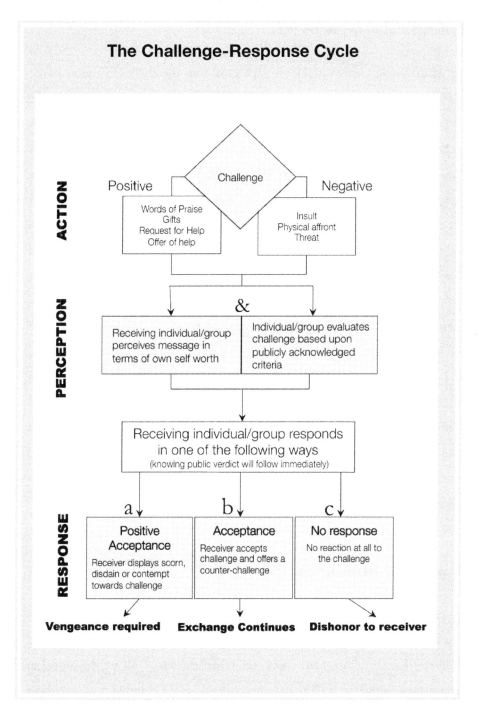

The Challenge-Response Cycle

ACTION

Challenge

Positive

Negative

Words of Praise
Gifts
Request for Help
Offer of help

Insult
Physical affront
Threat

PERCEPTION

&

Receiving individual/group perceives message in terms of own self worth

Individual/group evaluates challenge based upon publicly acknowledged criteria

Receiving individual/group responds in one of the following ways
(knowing public verdict will follow immediately)

RESPONSE

a

Positive Acceptance

Receiver displays scorn, disdain or contempt towards challenge

b

Acceptance

Receiver accepts challenge and offers a counter-challenge

c

No response

No reaction at all to the challenge

Vengeance required   **Exchange Continues**   **Dishonor to receiver**

** Adapted from Bruce J. Malina, *The New Testament World; Insights from Cultural Anthropology*, 3rd Edition, (Westminster John Knox Press, Louisville, KY, 2001)

Challenge and Response on 9/11

The World Trade Center attack on 9/11 illustrates the challenge and response model in several important ways. First, the 2001 attack served to redress the embarrassing loss of honor and status caused by the previous unsuccessful attack on the World Trade Center in 1993. When the 1993 conspirators failed to achieve the catastrophic results they had intended—toppling one tower onto the other, killing thousands of people—they and their fellow travelers were faced with the incentive to try again and thereby regain its lost honor. Second, the World Trade Center was both a prominent symbol of U.S. economic power and contained thousands of unprotected civilians. Third, while al-Qaeda seems to have gained little support for its attack in either the West or the Islamic world, it nevertheless managed to provoke the United States into counter-efforts that have been extremely costly, both in monetary terms as well as in terms of global standing and popularity. Al-Qaeda's challenge was met with a U.S. response that was (and continues to be) assessed and evaluated by the American public and world opinion, and this pattern is replicated in "war on terror" theaters of conflict around the globe. Since 2001, Al-Qaeda and the United States have been locked in a challenge-response cycle in which both seek to communicate with various audiences—Middle Eastern decision makers, American citizens, world leaders, to name a few—through terrorism and counter-terrorism efforts respectively.

Patron–Client relationships

The challenge and response model offers insight into not only the structures of intergroup conflict but also the mechanisms for creating and maintaining intergroup harmony. As noted above, the term "challenge" allows the model to account for positive as well as negative exchanges: for example, when terrorist groups seek out and approach potential patrons, and when states or larger terrorist groups seek out smaller terrorist groups as potential clients. Clients are individuals or groups that "have attached themselves to [powerful patrons] for reasons of ambition or in order to use them to protect or extend some particular interest."[5] A patron, therefore, is a person or group who protects and assists less powerful entities; in turn, the patrons expect their clients to reciprocate by acting in ways that sustain the patron's status and standing. It is "a two-way process—patron and client both need each other—and… it is also something that has to be worked at, attended to, over time."[6] Patron-client alignments are an important source of not only the means by which a group can accomplish its goals, but also of the self-perception of both parties, especially that of the client group. Thus, the SIT model is a useful tool for understanding patron-client relationships. In addition, there is the external, public evaluation of any given relationship, which places it within the challenge-response model.

> **client:** one that is under the protection of another
> *(Merriam-Webster.com*

> **p a t r o n :** o n e that uses wealth or influence to help an individual, an institution, or a cause
> *(Merriam-Webster.com*

The relationship between Hizbullah and Iran clearly illustrates these complex realities. The two are in an overt and very public patron-client relationship. As the patron, Iran supplies Hizbullah with funds, weapons, and the status that comes with the formal recognition by a powerful state. Hizbullah reciprocates through its allegiance to Iran's state ideology, and its public support for Iranian policy objectives, which extends Tehran's influence into the Levant. This relationship is not static, however, but constantly defined and redefined by positive public challenges: gifts and favors that need to be reciprocated in order to keep the relationship viable. Moreover, members of both groups continually

---

5 Roger Owen, *State, Power and Politics in the Making of the Modern Middle East* (London and New York: Routledge, 1999, 2nd ed.), p. 38.
6 Ibid.

assess and determine what sort of impact this relationship has on their social status, which is connected to (although not wholly defined by) the general public's evaluation and approval or disapproval of the relationship.

For instance, after Israel had destroyed Lebanese infrastructure in July 2006, Iran supplied Hizbullah with several hundred million U.S. dollars, mostly in cash, to facilitate reconstruction. The reconstruction money increased Hizbullah's standing in Lebanon, especially in the hardest hit communities. Hizbullah was expected, however, to use the money in ways that benefited not only itself, but also its patrons in Tehran. By distributing funds through Hizbullah, Iran was able to raise its level of popular support throughout the region, and to heighten already existing concerns among its enemies about the spread of Iranian influence in the Middle East. The standing of both Iran and Hizbullah in the eyes of their internal constituencies, as well as regional public opinion, was thus improved as both fulfilled their parts in the ongoing symbiotic patron-client relationship.

Honor-Shame

Honor and its counterpart, shame, have a pivotal social value in strongly group-oriented environments. Honor is a socially acknowledged claim to worth and status—prestige and standing—and can be both individual and collective. In a group setting, the honor associated with a group reflects on its members, and vice versa.[7]

> **honor:** respect that is given to someone who is admired; good reputation; good quality or character as judged by other people
>
> **shame:** a condition of humiliating disgrace or disrepute
>
> *(Merriam-Webster.com*

In environments where honor is a central concern, there is a constant dialectic between the idealized norms of socially sanctioned speech and behavior, on the one hand, and the way in which an individual or group seeks to reproduce those norms, on the other hand. In other words, codes of conduct, rules of engagement, and acting in accordance with the ideologies and principles of the group become matters of honor. When a person perceives that his or her actions do, in fact, reproduce those idealized norms, he or she expects other members of society to acknowledge this fact. This is equally true for groups: the group that believes it acts with honor expects to be recognized as honorable. Such an acknowledgment is a grant of honor.[8] As social scientist Bruce Malina writes,

> Honor as a pivotal value in a society implies a chosen way of conduct undertaken with a view to and because of entitlement to certain social treatment in return. Other people not only say that a person is honorable; they also treat that person in the way that honorable persons are treated.[9]

7　David Brannan and Anders Strindberg, *Social Identity Theory Module II: What is Social Identity Theory?* (Center for Homeland Defense and Security Online Learning Module, Naval Postgraduate School), https://www.chds.us/?media/openmedia&id=2919 (accessed 2-4-14).

8　Ibid.

9　Bruce J. Malina, *The New Testament World: Insights from Cultural Anthropology* (Louisville KY: Westminster-John Knox Press, 1993), p. 32.

The social process whereby honor is acquired, challenged, protected, or lost is the challenge and response cycle as it hinges on public communication or competition between individuals or groups that are, or consider themselves to be, each others' social equals. This interaction is necessarily public because honor is a socially acknowledged claim to status and all attempts to alter or maintain that status must be evaluated socially. As we discussed previously, even non-action is interpreted as a kind of response to a challenge, meriting a grant or a withdrawal of honor.

Physical space—one's body, territory, or property—is considered a symbolic repository of honor, and physical affronts and violence are symbolic violations of personal or intergroup boundaries. Thus, acts such as assassination, sabotage, terrorism, or territorial occupation are not only practical, but symbolic actions, "refus[als] to recognize...honor and prestige."[10] Such challenges require a response that seeks to evict or inflict damage on the intruder, reclaiming or restoring honor. Failure to redress the balance and restore the status quo ante may leave one's honor in a state of desecration, rendering oneself socially dishonored and dishonorable. On the other hand—and this is especially important when it comes to terrorist groups—the mere attempt to restore one's honor, even if ultimately unsuccessful, may restore of one's honor through the public perception and reassertion of oneself as a person or group of honor and integrity.[11]

Patron-client relations would be utterly unenforceable and practically impossible without a range of social norms and codes related to honor and shame. While they may be described sequentially in this book, they cannot be pried apart in reality. These relations, then, are based on a positive challenge within the challenge and response model. A gesture, petition, statement, or gift may initiate the patron-client process; thus, "there are no free gifts, just gifts which mark the

---

10 Ibid., p. 40.
11 David Brannan and Anders Strindberg, *Social Identity Theory Module II: What is Social Identity Theory?*

initiation or continuance of an ongoing reciprocal relationship."[12]

Limited Good

According to anthropologists studying Eastern Mediterranean communities, the patron-client relationship is intimately connected to the idea of the "limited good." Originally informed by the social realities of peasant society, this idea hinges on the assumption that social, economic, and natural resources exist only in limited quantity and are

> **limited good:** is a concept from anthropology describing the theory commonly held in traditional societies, that there is a limited amount of "good" to go around. In other words, the amount of land, money, etc. available is held to be finite, so every time one person profits, another loses.
>
> *(wikipedia.org)*

always in short supply. Even as Eastern Mediterranean societies have developed in terms of societal structures, modes of production, and so forth, certain social and material goods continue to exist only in finite quantities and are therefore subject to intense competition. In the Palestinian context, for instance, physical space—land—has not only been a limited good, it has also been invaded by an outgroup. This invasion of physical space is thus a double challenge to Palestinian national honor: physical and symbolic.

Importantly, honor itself is considered a limited good in the Eastern Mediterranean. As noted above, the purpose of the challenge and response cycle is to establish or regain honor. This is important because honor is social capital, and as such it is considered a limited resource. Within the competitive and comparative challenge and response model, the quest for honor is a zero-sum game: your gain of honor is my loss, and vice versa.[13]

---

12 Bruce J. Malina, *The New Testament World*, p. 101.
13 David Brannan and Anders Strindberg, *Social Identity Theory Module II: What is Social Identity Theory?*

Limited Good

On September 9, 1993, Yasir Arafat, Chairman of the Palestine Liberation Organization (PLO) and Israeli Prime Minister Yitzhak Rabin exchanged letters of recognition. This was the overt beginning of the Oslo Process, but it was also the result of lengthy top secret negotiations. On the Palestinian side, these negotiations involved less than a dozen of Arafat's closest aides and associates. The leaders of the other PLO factions, who considered themselves Arafat's equals, found out about it together with the rest of the world.

The PLO opposition factions were furious, condemning the Oslo accords and vowing to derail the peace process. Within a month they had established their own umbrella organization that went on to reaffirm the continued need to liberate Palestine "from the river Jordan to the Mediterranean Sea," declaring that "the present PLO leadership does not represent the Palestinian people, nor does it express its views or aspirations."[14]

This was a political response to a political event, designed to counter Arafat's attack on the other Palestinian leaders' collective honor. Even though Arafat had long been "first among equals" in the PLO, he had now publicly violated a colleague contract, seeking to establish himself as sole patron of the

---

14 "Declaration of the Alliance of Palestinian Forces," Damascus, 6 January 1994.

Palestinian people at his colleagues' expense. This shamed them in front of the people: not only were they kept in the dark, they were left out of an informational loop of which the ultimate outgroup—Israel—was very much a part. Because the public loss of honor means a loss of social capital (which itself is political currency), the opposition sought to redeem and reassert themselves by counterchallenging Arafat's social status. The main purpose of the new alliance was not so much to wrest power from the PLO/Palestinian Authority leadership as to publicly defy it. For the next several years, the PLO opposition consistently and studiously promoted itself as the militant voice of the disaffected, the steadfast defender of national unity and honor, and of the right to military struggle—against Israel and "Arafatism." Defying Arafat became as important to their identity as fighting against Israel, as it proved them men of honor, which was nothing less than an existential requirement.

Chapter Summary:

- Within a patron-client relationship, the patron provides its client with protection and assets, while the client, in exchange, gives its service and support.

- The challenge and response cycle consists of three components: the challenge (an action to statement on the part of a group), perception (the way that the challenged group and the larger public perceive this action), and response (the challenged group's reaction and the public's perception of this response).

- A challenge can be negative or positive.

- Both honor and shame are publicly performed and evaluated, and are acquired, tested, maintained, or lost during the challenge and response cycle.

- If a resource is considered a "limited good," it means that, whether it is tangible (like land) or intangible (like status), one group's gain is another's loss, and vice versa.

- These analytical markers work in concert with each other and can be useful for analyzing terrorism with an SIT framework.

Analytical Markers

5

Religion: Just Another Group?

Overview

Having examined terrorism as public communication and terrorist groups as social groups, we can ask whether religious groups can be analyzed using the same method used to examine the others—SIT. Religiously motivated terrorist groups are commonly assumed to be exotic—"other-worldly" and focused on something beyond the here and now—and their actions and behaviors therefore somehow different from those of "regular" social groups. Nevertheless, like their secular counterparts, religious terrorist groups have strong ingroup boundaries, explicit enemies (both temporally and cosmically), and operate fairly consistently in accordance with the challenge and response model. The SIT model and the analytical markers described in previous chapters are helpful tools for understanding religious groups, and can allow the analyst to avoid the potential bias issues inherent in some of the more common analytical frameworks in the literature.

Focus Questions:

- What are some of the common misconceptions and intellectual hurdles an analyst might face when examining religious terrorist groups?

- What are the factors that can lead to intensified boundaries between ingroups and outgroups when examining religious groups?

- Why is context still critical when analyzing the actions of a particular religious group?

- How do SIT and the analytical markers enable an analyst to use other traditional prescriptive terrorism models (eg. rational actor, instrumental and organizational) more effectively?

The socially constructed boundaries and strong ingroup cohesion found in religious terrorist groups seem to baffle many analysts. That need not be the case. Practitioners around the world have often seen or experienced the reality of ingroup cohesion in ways that many traditional academics have not. One need go no further than the local street gang or outlaw motorcycle club to recognize how ingroup cohesion and boundaries are set and enforced through both explicit and unspoken means.[1] The practitioner can easily transfer such insights to the study of groups that use religious mandates, language, and authority. While their ideas and ideals may be very different, and the intergroup boundaries and

> **ingroup cohesion:** a group is said to be in a state of cohesion when its members possess bonds linking them to one another and to the group as a whole. Although cohesion is a multi-factored process, it can be broken down into four main components: social relations, task relations, perceived unity, and emotions. Members of strongly cohesive groups are more inclined to participate readily and to stay with the group.
>
> *(wikipedia.org)*

ingroup cohesion may be even stronger and more pronounced in religious terrorist groups, the mechanisms whereby they are established and maintained are essentially the same.

It is important to note that those we designate "religious terrorists" tend to form an extremely small subset of a larger religious community. For instance, Lebanese Hizbullah are comprised of Lebanese Shi'a, but they do not represent all Shi'a Muslims or even all Shi'a Muslims in Lebanon. Similarly, while Pastor Thom

---

1　For an insider's perspective on how this occurs within outlaw motorcycle clubs, see Ralph "Sonny" Barger with Keith and Kent Zimmerman, *Hell's Angel*, (New York: William Morrow, 2000). For a gang studies perspective, see Thomas Barker, *Biker Gangs and Organized Crime* (Newark, NJ: Matthew Bender and Company, Inc., 2007). For an investigative journalistic approach illuminating similar issues see, Yves Lavigne, *Hell's Angels: Three Can Keep A Secret If Two Are Dead*, (New York: Lyle Stuart, 1987).

Robb of Harrison, Arkansas claims to speak for Christian believers in general, his particular racially focused Christian Identity Theology limits his authority to his local Knights Party of the Ku Klux Klan. To assume that any religious terrorist speaks or acts on behalf of an entire religion is to commit the fallacy of composition; this will always lead the analyst to inaccuracies that may in turn lead to operational overreach. In order to ensure or enforce group cohesion, politically active religious groups of all types tend to hold to a particular and sometimes idiosyncratic understanding of the broader religious framework within which they exist. These groups typically form around important local issues that may or may not be religious—they may be economic, political, ethnic, or nationalistic—but that are understood, explained, and addressed within a specific theological framework.

At the most basic level, religious groups are just that: groups. Both SIT and the other analytical markers that have been discussed throughout this book can be as readily applied to these groups as they are to secular groups. The analyst must not let words like "religious" and "theologically motivated" move him or her to abandon a method that has proven useful to group study.

TAKENOTE

The analyst should remember that religion, theology, and faith are all very different concepts.

- Religion has to do with the organization of beliefs and people.

- Faith is the personal belief of the individual.

- Theology is the study of God and is often related to a particular understanding of religious text.

With that said, there are a few additional concepts that need to be considered in order to make the distinctions between religious and secular terrorism clear, which will in turn increase analytical accuracy. Although there is no universally accepted or absolute definition of the term religion, it can be described generally as the organization of beliefs and world views in relation to some supernatural reality. Thus, when thinking about religious terrorism, the definitional imprecision that is a constant challenge in the effort to define and understand terrorism in general increases as we seek to understand religious terrorism in particular.

Religion informs and structures a person's understanding of who she is and her relationship to others. This is true of the group as well as the individual: a religion sets up boundaries that establish similarities within a group and differences from other groups. A nonpolitical example of this can be seen within Christianity

TAKENOTE

Warning!!
Labeling a group a Christian, Jewish, or Islamic terrorist organization should immediately alert the informed practitioner that the group is using certain theological concepts or religious structures, but that its actions *do not*, therefore, represent the broader religion.

in the United States, where Evangelical Christians are often quick to note they are quite different from Roman Catholic Christians, and vice versa. Individuals on both sides of this Christian divide are frequently willing to argue that the other is not "really" Christian. This tendency—a function of ingroup/outgroup identity formation—exists within most religions.

In other words, group identification can be both personal and collective, defining the difference between "me" and "you," as well as "us" and "them." Jonathan Fox has suggested that religion in particular also fulfills four important social functions:

1. Provides a meaningful framework for understanding the world.
2. Provides rules and standards of behavior that link individual actions and goals to this meaningful framework.
3. Links individuals to a greater whole, sometimes providing formal institutions which help to define and organize that whole.
4. Possesses the ability to legitimize actions and institutions.[2]

---

2 Jonathan Fox, "Do Religious Institutions Support Violence or the Status Quo?", *Studies in Conflict and Terrorism,* Vol. 22: Issue 2 (1999), pp.119-139.

The importance of text

Religious beliefs are often founded on sacred texts.[3] A group's interpretation of such texts takes place in social, political, and cultural contexts, which often have profound impact on the understanding of the text. Different sects or denominations within a religion may point to exactly the same portion of exactly the same text to justify very different "truths" within their particular group.

Such differences in interpretations can give rise to, not only different sects of the same religion, but to different (though related) religions entirely. On a macro-level, Judaism is based on a Jewish interpretation of the Hebrew Bible, which comprises much of the text that Christians refer to as the "Old Testament" as part of the Christian Bible. Many of the themes (and, indeed, characters and events) addressed in the Hebrew Bible are also found in the Qur'an, the foundational sacred text of Islam. Judaism, Christianity, and Islam are known as the "Abrahamic religions" because they all trace their lineage back to Abraham, and they primarily focus on the interpretation of their respective, overlapping and (in some aspects) substantially similar religious texts. In contrast, though Hinduism and Buddhism have important religious texts, they do not place the same emphasis on textual authority as the Abrahamic religions.

Abrahamic Faiths

---

3   For instance, the Qu'ran is foundational to Islam, the Torah to Judaism, and the Bible to Christianity.

Yet, while primary figures, themes, and events described in the Abrahamic texts may be similar, the theological imperatives that are produced within each tradition can be vastly different. This is especially true in cases of intergroup conflict, when references to a similar heritage become points of conflict, rather than dialogue. As Mateus de Azevedo suggests:

> Fundamentalist interpretations of religion tend to disproportionately highlight the differences between faiths. However, Christianity and Islam share many things in common, even if fundamentalists are not willing to admit this fact. For instance, Christians and Muslims are both monotheistic, i.e. they believe in one God; both belong to the same Abrahamic category of religions, which also includes Judaism; both believe in the immortality of the soul, in the rewards or punishments in the afterlife, according to the merits or demerits achieved in this life; both believe in the reality of prayer as a method of communicating with God; both believe in moral law; both believe in the importance of the practice of the virtues, especially humility and generosity, and many other common aspects which the fundamentalist approach tends to overlook.[4]

Despite such commonalities, in a context of fear and conflict, one group may view other groups as "outsiders." The differences between the ingroup and outgroups are often seen as clear-cut and absolute, and delineated by the Word of God—or, to be more analytically precise, the ingroup's interpretation of the Word of God. In this context, similarities recede into the background. The resultant theologies form strong ingroup boundaries that determine who is in and who is out of the group.

---

4   Mateus Soares De Azevedo, *Men of a Single Book: Fundamentalism in Islam, Christianity, and Modern Thought* (Bloomington, IN, World Wisdom, 2010) p. 23.

Often in a religious terrorist organization, everyone outside the theologically established boundaries become, to varying degrees, the enemy. In some cases, the enmity is rhetorical, while in other cases the enmity is such that it leads to violence. In both cases, however, the enemy is ascribed an identity by the religious ingroup; this means that the outgroup's beliefs and actions are interpreted against

> **enmity:** the state or feeling of being actively opposed or hostile to someone or something.
> *(oxforddictionaries.com)*

the background of the ingroup's identity and theology. For instance, "seed-line" Christian Identity Theology views Jewish people as the literal offspring of satan, and consequently interprets all actions by or on behalf of Jews as satanic (see Alan Berg example described at the end of this chapter). This in turn tends to lead to confirmation bias—one sees what one expects to see—and is conducive to creating and maintaining intractable conflict. In all of this, religious terrorist groups are not dissimilar to secular terrorist groups. A major difference, however, is that the "enemy other" is not only thought to be the enemy of the religious ingroup, but also the enemy of God. This is important because the extension of such a view of the enemy is that compromise, settlement, or negotiation are seen as apostasy—treason against God.

Members of all religious groups are motivated to maintain the group's socially constructed boundaries.[5] Again, this is especially true in situations of conflict. Such boundaries are defined and maintained by the confluence of any number of factors. For instance, the interpretation of sacred text through accepted ingroup hermeneutics is very important, but not the only important factor to consider. Textual interpretation will take place in conjunction with unfolding political realities on the ground, the impact of historical factors, features of the cultural milieu, and so forth. Focus on one factor to the exclusion of other important factors—such as the common claim that Islamic terrorism can be explained with reference to some key proof texts in the Qur'an—will inhibit analytical accuracy. In fact, the credibility of this one-dimensional approach is shattered by one very simple question: why doesn't everyone who views a particular text as authoritative behave in the same way? That is to say, why are not all Muslims suicide bombers? Why are not all Christians vandalizing abortion clinics or killing doctors who perform abortions? The foundational text on its own does not explain these actions; we have to look to the interpretation of text, and the context of that interpretation, in order to drill down into the phenomenon.

Often the actions of terrorist groups appear irrational to those outside the group while, to those on the inside, the same actions are likely to appear absolutely rational. This is not unique to terrorist groups. Not unlike the ingroup coherence, identity, and loyalty that develops within small combat units, terrorist groups develop particular perspectives about what is rational, commendable, altruistic, and heroic within a context of urgent need. Take, for instance, the case of U.S. Army Private First Class Ross A. McGinnis. PFC McGinnis was posthumously awarded the country's highest military award, the Congressional Medal of Honor, after he threw himself on a fragmentation grenade, allowing his four colleagues

---

5 For instance The Catholic church has written boundaries that distinguish it from Protestant religious groups. See, http://www.vatican.va/archive/ENG0015/_INDEX.HTM for a Catholic perspective. Or, http://www.pcanet.org/general/cof_contents.htm for a Protestant view specifically counter to the Catholic perspective given above.

to escape. According to everyone at the scene, McGinnis had time to escape but chose death in order to protect his colleagues.[6] Those outside the very tight ingroup that is formed by soldiers in battle may well see McGinnis' sacrifice as irrational, unnecessary, and incomprehensible. Yet viewed within the very real socially constructed reality of small units operating under fire, the bravery of PFC McGinnis was the supreme act of camaraderie.

Similarly, the ingroup's socially constructed perspective on theological realities and requirements may be difficult for those who are outside the group to fully understand due to their different frames of reference. This is true also for ideological realities and requirements that are not shared by an observer. For instance, a terrorist group's unwillingness to bend to the overwhelming power of the state with which they are in conflict may be coherent and sensible to those inside the terrorist group while appearing hopeless, desperate, and irrational to outside observers. Examples of this are easily seen within the Palestinian/Israeli conflict. Many outside the conflict see the actions of Hamas or the Palestinian Islamic Jihad as irrational given the state of Israel's overwhelming military capabilities and U.S. political support. Yet viewed from the inside, these groups feel assured of victory by God (in much the same way as Marxist-Leninist terrorist groups feel assured of victory by history) because they are fighting for the land and the people in a way that is pleasing to God. Thus, what looks irrational from the etic perspective is understood as fully rational within the emic framework

---

6   See http://www.army.mil/medalofhonor/mcginnis/citation/index.html.

Guides for analysis, not determination of action

It is important to remember that none of the frameworks for analysis described in this book are determinative; that is, they do not describe patterns of behavior into which the groups are locked (e.g. "if Group A does X then it follows that Group B will do Y" or "if group A believes X then it will necessarily do Y"). Terrorists are rational actors and their actions are internally coherent and knowable in context. This insight allows the analyst to effectively use traditional analytical frames, such as instrumental or organizational perspectives. When used in conjunction with the analytical markers we have discussed previously in this book, SIT allows us to use traditional evaluative tools while at the same time allowing our analysis to be more culturally relevant and analytically precise.

Organizational models and internally coherent and socially constructed reality of violent sub-national groups

Terrorist, insurgent, or extremist groups are not only groups, they are also organizations. Their context is radically different than most other organizations due to fact that the use of violence, the need for clandestinity, and the threat of death are important influences on terrorist group thinking and action.[7] Nevertheless, they have structural and management needs and requirements that are similar to many other organizations, and important analytical insights can be gleaned by taking this seriously.

---

7   For interesting insights on the role and impact of clandestinity on terrorist groups, see David Tucker, *Illuminating the Dark Arts of War* (New York: Continuum International Publishing Group), p. 57.

For instance ...

In October 2005, the Director of National Intelligence released a letter from then second-in-command of al-Qaeda Central (AQC), Ayman al-Zawahiri to the head of al-Qaeda in Iraq (AQI), Abu Musab al-Zarqawi. The lengthy letter was framed in theological terms, but nevertheless betrayed the organizational concerns of AQC with the tactics of al-Qaeda in Iraq (AQI).[8] The letter directed the subordinate AQI leader al-Zarqawi to address issues that had become concerns for AQC. These included the graphic "slaughter" of hostages, the targeting of Shi'a, the possibility for non-Iraqi leadership within AQI, and a request from al-Zawahiri for payment of $100,000 from AQI to AQC.[9] In analyzing the letter, contextual issues related to theology, Quranic precepts, and nationality are helpful when organized within an SIT framework—yet awareness of management needs within a structured organization is helpful for understanding the nature of the exchange.

Instrumental violence: the dangers of mistaking sub-national violent groups for States

In order to distinguish political violence from criminal or other forms of violence, it is important to understand the instrumentality of terrorism. When a terrorist organization attacks a particular target, the action they take is itself an act of communication. Bruce Hoffman argues convincingly that terrorist group violence is important for internal reasons as well as for its external uses.

> The exact purpose of these communications can vary, depending upon the message and the target audience(s) to whom it is directed. It can be didactic—designed to inform, educate, solicit support (whether material, financial, or spiritual), and ultimately rally the masses behind the insurgents or terrorists.[10]

It is important to note that these are all rational and goal-oriented actions; specific means calibrated to achieve specific ends. Hoffman goes on to identify

---

8   Susan B. Glasser and Walter Pincus, "Seized Letter Outlines al-Qaeda Goals in Iraq," *The Washington Post*, October 12, 2005, accessed at; http://www.washingtonpost.com/wp-dyn/content/article/2005/10/11/AR2005101101353.html.

9   For an English translation of the letter, see http://www.ctc.usma.edu/wp-content/uploads/2013/10/Zawahiris-Letter-to-Zarqawi-Translation.pdf.

10 Bruce Hoffman, *Inside Terrorism*, p. 41.

that the internal utility of terrorist violence is the way that it maintains social boundaries and reinforces ingroup cohesion.

> Finally, it can serve an entirely internal function—what has been termed "auto-propaganda"—when it is directed toward members of the terrorist group in order to strengthen morale, dampen dissent, or justify and legitimate or explain particularly controversial decisions or operations.[11]

al-Qaeda letter continued ...

Returning to the letter from Zawahiri to Zarqawi discussed above, we can see instrumental as well as organizational goals. Consider that terrorist organization's use violence as a mode of communication. When ideally calibrated, the level of violence will terrorize the outgroup while garnering support from constituents of the nominal ingroup. When that violence is not properly calibrated, it can have the opposite effect. This imbalance is what we see when Zawahiri challenges the AQI leader to stop the "slaughter" of captives. While Zawahiri sees the actions as theologically justified, he calls on Zarqawi to stop publicizing the gruesome beheadings because supporters of al-Qaeda's cause are turned off by the gruesome and graphic nature of the violence.[12]

As Hoffman explains, violence is both the method and the means of terrorist communication, which in turn is an example of why terrorist violence must be considered rational action. This is true for both religious and secular groups. This means, as we have noted in earlier chapters, that by looking at the violence in context, we can better interpret the message or messages. The most challenging part of the equation is establishing a relevant contextual framework. If we place the violence in an irrelevant or partially relevant contextual framework, rational and calculated actions may seem irrational or crazy. If the group under analysis is a religious group, there is really no difference in how the analytical framework is applied, there are simply additional factors that must be accounted for as relevant context (e.g., the importance of doing God's will, fear of divine punishment, apocalyptic visions, etc.).

---

11 Ibid, p.199.
12 For an English translation of the letter, see http://www.ctc.usma.edu/wp-content/

Examining Alan Berg's murder using SIT

Christian Identity theology has been central to many religious extremist groups in the United States, Britain, and Canada. It is counter to what many Christians see as "authentic" Christianity, yet Christian Identity theology adherents use the same Biblical text that mainline Christians use. From their particular interpretive framework they derive very different theological positions, which are often racially focused.[13] Groups subscribing to this theology include well-known organizations such as the Aryan Nations, the Covenant Sword, and the Arm of the Lord (CSA), as well as some KKK groups.[14] Some of these groups have used violence to spread their message.

One of the central issues of Christian Identity theology is the idea that there is a "hidden Israel' in the white European races; they are the direct descendants and heirs of the tribes of Israel described in the Old Testament. The so-called "two seed" forms of Identity theology look to Genesis 3:15 as Scriptural foundation for that perspective.[15] These "seed-line" Christian Identity groups claim not only that white people are the "true" Israelites (or God's chosen people), but that Jews are the literal offspring of Satan and that all non-whites are subhuman descendants of animals.

---

uploads/2013/10/Zawahiris-Letter-to-Zarqawi-Translation.pdf.

13 The classic work on the roots of Christian Identity theology is Michael Barkun, *Religion and the Racist Right* (Chapel Hill: The University of North Carolina Press, 1997). For further depth on how various groups have used the theology to define ingroup boundaries and cohesion, see David Brannan, *Violence, Terrorism and the Role of Theology : Repentant and Rebellious Christian Identity*, (St. Andrews, University of St. Andrews, 2007) PhD dissertation.

14 Christian Identity theology is a religious belief system and is unrelated to the analytical framework used throughout this work called Social Identity Theory.

15 For the most in depth Christian Identity explanation of the Two-Seeds position, see Dan Gayman, *The Two Seeds of Genesis 3:15* (Schell City MO: The Church of Israel, 1977).

Looking at Aryan Nations we can see that ingroup identity is affirmed not only on the basis of race—Aryan Nation members must be white—but also on an acceptance of the group's core belief system, seed-line Christian Identity Theology. Group boundaries are in part set by the religious text as interpreted within the group's particular frame for understanding. Much of the interaction between law enforcement and the group is seen as a negative honor challenge against the ingroup, as the government system is viewed as a structure intended to subvert their religious views. While government officials may legitimize their actions with reference to the law and societal structures, members of Aryan Nations presuppose those structures to be an anti-Christian attempt to defend members of their enemy outgroups: non-whites, Jews, and white people that do not adhere to Identity Theology, whom they see as traitors against the truth.

Maintaining views that most modern Americans see as outrageous, anti-social, and dangerous racist beliefs in the face of societal norms is in and of itself a method of honor maintenance for the group. By not bending to socially dominant views of Biblical text, racial equality, or mainstream Christianity, the small ingroup reaffirms cohesion and commitment as the "righteous remnant." Though their views seem preposterous, alien, and offensive when viewed from the etic perspective, members' theological and social positions are completely coherent and authoritative for the ingroup. Importantly, if we take these beliefs seriously, we can identify and analyze vital pieces of information that decision makers can use to prevent, deter, or respond to these kinds of groups more effectively.

In June 1984 Denver, Colorado, shock radio host Alan Berg was shot to death. Berg was Jewish and had spoken out against, argued with, and belittled white supremacy and Christian Identity groups on his show. Jean Craig, David Lane, Bruce Pierce, and Richard Scutari were indicted for crimes related to Berg's killing, though none of them were convicted of the homicide. All four men were members of a splinter group from Aryan Nations known as The Order, which was based in seed-line Christian Identity theology.[16] Lane claimed to have called and baited Berg on his radio program about Christian Identity and racial issues, and he and Pierce were convicted of racketeering, conspiracy, and violating Berg's civil rights. Lane was sentenced to 190 years in prison and died in 2007. Pierce was sentenced to 252 years and died in a federal prison in 2010.[17]

Even against such a brief background on the Aryan Nations and The Order, SIT is a useful framework for teasing out important aspects of group dynamics and organizing them in a way that creates useful analysis. Virtually every report or article can be similarly distilled into a systematic and organized understanding of key issues that are relevant to practitioner oriented analysis.

By using the categories of SIT and the analytical markers to organize the facts, we can account for common group elements or actions in a structured and contextually informed fashion. Breaking the information into the various component parts is key to providing coherent and systematic insight upon which to base actions or policies. But it is important to remember that our efforts are not aimed at articulating the framework. The framework is a tool and a means, not a product. The components and markers are important and useful, helping us uncover contextual and analytical insights through an organized and repeatable method, but are not particularly helpful if the framework rather than the analysis becomes the focus. That analytical product always centers on the research subject—the terrorist group or event—while the SIT categories and markers provide us a solid method that gives structure and rigor. We build upon this effort in the next and final chapter.

---

16 For a detailed recounting of the Order's rise and fall, see Kevin Flynn and Gary Gerhardt, *The Silent Brotherhood*, (New York, Signet, 1990).

17 See Howard Pankratz, "Neo-Nazi gunman in Alan Berg's murder dies in prison" *Denver Post*, August 17, 2010. http://www.denverpost.com/ci_15805243#ixzz2uHCfmAWf (accessed 2-23-14).

Applying the Framework

Key issues to identify within the framework are:

Ingroup: Those that held a racial and theological belief system based on Christian Identity theology. Specifically, the group known as the Order, they were a criminal and terrorist organization spawned by Aryan Nations.

Outgroup: This follows from the identity of the ingroup: Jews, non-whites, and all whites who did not accept their Christian Identity theology perspectives. The enormity of the outgroup serves to bolster the ingroup's view as a righteous remnant before God.

Patron/Client relationships: Christian Identity adherents are involved in multiple patron-client relationships. The foremost relationship is between the believer and his or her understanding of what is required by God in order to be an honorable person. Another relates to temporal organizational leadership—Richard Butler of Aryan Nations and Robert Matthews filled the patron role for most within the Order.

Challenge/Response: Each interaction between the ingroup and various outgroups presents a type of honor challenge. For instance, the claim by Lane to have baited Berg on the air was viewed by Lane as a positive honor challenge toward his ingroup, improving his own standing with his peers, while simultaneously constituting a negative honor challenge against Jews in general and Berg in particular. The killing of Berg was the ultimate negative honor challenge by the ingroup.

Honor/Shame: The group perceived their honor to have been challenged by the multicultural structures of society that denied white racial superiority and, more specifically, by Berg's assertions on his radio show.

Limited Good: Their ability, real or perceived, to influence the public sphere with what the ingroup believed to be a positive view of white supremacy and Christian Identity beliefs.

Ingroup cohesion: The killing of Berg was a publicly observed and evaluated honor challenge which potentially served to either increase ingroup cohesion (seen as a unifying action by those who believed the killing to be in the interest of the ingroup) or to decrease ingroup cohesion (by those who believed that physical rather than rhetorical attacks against the outgroup weakened the ingroup).

Chapter Summary:

- Because religious groups are just that—groups—they can be analyzed using methods that measure and assess the dynamics of other, non-religious groups, including SIT and the other analytical markers to which we have been previously introduced.

- As described by Jonathan Fox, religion fulfills four important social functions: it provides a meaningful framework for understanding the world; provides rules and standards for behavior that link individual actions and goals to this meaningful framework; it links individuals to a greater whole, sometimes providing formal institutions which help to define and organize the whole; and it possesses the ability to legitimize actions and institutions.

- Many religions center on the interpretation of a sacred text, although members of the same religion can come to very different interpretations of the same text, and thus have very different outlooks on the world. As such. members of the same religion cannot be arbitrarily grouped together, despite some shared beliefs.

- Ingroup dynamics allow members to rationalize and justify actions that may not appear coherent or sensible to outsiders; these dynamics are even more powerful in a clandestine environment, or when the views held and espoused by the group are not acceptable according to the social "mainstream."

- Terrorist violence is a specific goal in itself, but it is more powerful as a very public method of communication between the terrorist group, the political institution they are resisting (for example, the United States government), and the larger public.

Religion, Just Another Group?

6

Using the Tools

Overview

This section provides you, the analyst, with some final observations and considerations as you begin to apply the frameworks and markers introduced in this book to your actual work in the field. Sources are deconstructed and outlined carefully to help the analyst to develop, use, and exploit them effectively in an unclassified environment. The SIT framework and other analytical markers that have been introduced in this book are applied to real-life scenarios, illustrating the various ways in which these tools can be used effectively; this includes sources as easily accessible and readily available as FaceBook, Twitter, blogs and other social media. We hope that you will refer back to these these varied examples as a reference guide as the need arises.

Focus Questions:

- How does the application of an systematic framework (like SIT) enable the analyst to deliver diagnostic products that can provide real value to practitioners and policy makers involved in counter-terrorism efforts?

- What are a few contextual factors that should be considered in order to produce more accurate analysis?

- What factors can affect the accuracy of sources you may use in your analysis, and how can the analyst best protect him/herself from imprecision?

- How can the SIT framework be applied to varied source materials?

Now it is time to put all of the important components of this analytical framework together. An analytical product, whether it deals with a group, an individual, or an idea, is not a profile. This is important to keep in mind. A profile is about what happened and when it happened: dates and facts, names of leaders, relations with other groups, etc. Analysis goes a step further: it takes the facts of the profile, places them within an analytical framework, and then asks more "abstract" questions: why was there this upsurge in violence? Why did the group emerge when it did? Why did it expand? Why did its leader make a particular statement at a particular time? Why did Group A establish relations with group B? Why did it identify groups C and D as key enemies?

To put it another way: dates, events, and other facts are the basic building blocks of good analysis, while the analytical framework is the scaffolding that gives shape to the building. In an analytical product, you look at the facts, alignments, the timeline, and so forth, and then ask: "given the assumptions of the analytical framework, what might explain that the group made this particular choice at this particular time?" The basic assumptions of your analytical framework provide you with a roadmap to use as you go about looking for the hidden connections that can be either the underlying reasons for a particular action or statement, or their implications and effects. These analytical assumptions enhance your vision, allowing you to keep an eye out for both causes and effects. If you find that a group acquired a new patron, won or lost a major battle, or did anything else of political importance, then you should ask yourself how this new relationship or situation might have affected the group in terms of ideology, tactics, targeting, relations with other groups, or many other factors—and then ask why it was done.

Using SIT to effectively craft a group analysis out of a group profile requires subtly weaving its theoretical assumptions into your text, rather than stating them bluntly and going through, point by point, how they apply to the group. No policy maker wants to read a case study proving the accuracy of your analytical framework—they want to read a narrative about the specific group, person, or issue that you have been called upon to analyze. Let the framework blend into the background of your narrative, giving shape to your facts. Even if you merely mention it in a footnote, it can still be used to frame your entire study.

Remember also that analytical integrity requires the analyst to look actively for facts that contradict his or her assumptions. As we mentioned earlier, bias is natural and unavoidable. It only becomes a problem—a matter of intellectual dishonesty, in fact—when it causes the analyst to ignore facts contradicting that bias. The same applies to your analytical framework. Once you apply it, if you discover relevant facts that do not correspond with the framework, you must nevertheless account for those facts. Adjust the framework—it is not set in stone—but be consistent in your factual accounts. Discovery and understanding are, after all, the whole point of analysis.

Contextualization

Whether you need to analyze a terrorist attack, a statement by a terrorist leader, or the trajectory of a terrorist group, context and sources are key. As you consider context, remember that it is not a finite and tangible "thing" to be uncovered. Contextualization is an analytical process that creates an important element of the analytical product: a relevant context for your specific study. That product may require revision the next time you do analysis. As discussed earlier, context is not only multilayered and complex, but also fluid and specific—it changes over time, from place to place, and often from situation to situation. This makes contextualization time-consuming, which is precisely why so much of what passes for terrorism analysis in the public square today neglects to do it properly, and is consequently of very little use.

Often our analysis of a terrorist attack starts with the question, "what does it mean?" We seek to understand who the attacker is, why a specific target was chosen, the group's current trajectory, and where or what it is likely to target next. From the position of the analyst, this is backwards. Ideally, we would want to know the groups, their objectives, and the environments in which they function before we begin analysis; unfortunately, this is a luxury we do not often have. In order to produce accurate analysis, however, it is necessary to study the various groups and cultural settings, political relationships, ideological concerns, and theological commitments that blend into the intricate context within which our analysis must take place. This cannot be emphasized enough: *contexts are essential to understanding the issues you seek to analyze, whatever those issues are.*

For instance, if you are going to conduct analysis on a specific topic—say, suicide attacks by a particular Salafi-jihadi group such as al-Shabaab in Somalia— it is never too soon to begin considering the various contextual issues surrounding the group. Context is a multilayered, complex, and fluid set of features that make up the environment in which a group operates—but it must nevertheless be specific to that group. Here are some of the factors you might consider:

Specific national/regional politics. The relationships, agendas, and conditions that affect al-Shabaab in Somalia are not the same as those affecting Lashkar e-Tayiba in Pakistan, even though both are Salafi-jihadi. While theological precepts may be similar or identical, the political issues and pressures are not.

Specific theological markers. Salafi-jihadi groups draw on Salafi-jihadi theology. Generalizing about Islam, or the ideas of some theological subset within Islam that is not Salafi-jihadi, will set your analysis on the wrong path. Remember, theological differences are often extremely important for tactical as well as strategic objectives.

Specific social and cultural group settings. Which ingroup/outgroup and/or patron/client relationships are significant enough to affect the thought, rhetoric, and actions of a specific group? These will be unique for almost every group on the planet, and are of crucial operational importance.

Specific group objectives. What does the group claim to seek on the ground? How does this fit with its ideological/theological rhetoric? Is there a gap between rhetoric and action? For the counter-terrorism analyst, actions almost always speak louder than words. If there is a discrepancy between actions and rhetoric, that may be significant in and of itself.

For instance, we may learn something about the tactic of suicide bombing in general by studying the group that has made the most successful use of it, the Liberation Tigers of Tamil Eelam (LTTE) in Sri Lanka. However, apart from some technological and hardware aspects, studying the LTTE's use of suicide bombings would teach us nothing about the tactical or strategic use of suicide bombings in Somalia because the political, social, cultural, ideological, and theological contexts that give meaning to terrorist actions are very different. Similarly, learning about the use of suicide attacks by al-Qaeda in Iraq will give us comparative insight into the actions of that particular Salafi-jihadi group, but those insights are not fully transferable to an analysis of al-Shabaab; what is politically and culturally possible, permissible, or desirable in the Somali context is different from that of Iraq. On the other hand, learning about Somali politics, culture, and society will provide a local context for Somalia, but will not inform us about the global affiliations, allegiances, and motivating factors that are part of al-Shabaab's Salafi-jihadi ideology.

Learning about various contextual issues makes your future analysis easier and more exact. Although it will need to be updated and adapted, the next time you do analysis of al-Shabaab, part of your work is already done. One of the authors of this book has spent a lot of time researching Palestinian groups while another has focused much of his research on theologically-motivated, Right-wing extremists in the United States. In very different settings, the Middle East and the Midwest, each of us looked for the same contextual and structural factors, broadly speaking: ingroups and outgroups, patrons and clients, limited resources, significant social and political issues, ideology, theology, and so on. Clearly the specifics of Middle Eastern cultural contexts cannot be applied to groups from South Missouri any more than the specifics of Christian Identity theology would be helpful to explain the actions of Hamas. Yet the frames, structures, and relationships that helped us construct analysis were essentially the same.

We each looked at the actions and statements of the groups we sought to understand, examining the texts they produced, the interviews they gave, and the promotional material they put out. We spoke with the leaders, members, and acquaintances of these groups, as well as of groups opposed to them. We spent time with government officials and private stakeholders, always seeking to understand the context surrounding the group and their actions. We asked questions about bias: our own bias and that of the sources we used, insofar as it might affect our analysis. Of course, we also looked at existing academic and practitioner oriented literature, which is generally the starting point for research and analysis. In our literature searches, we were not only looking for facts, but also attuning ourselves to how those facts were pieced together. Similarly, we looked at news reports, both written and broadcast, carefully paying attention to editorial positions and the editing of primary source material such as documents, interviews, and videos.

Sources

The accuracy of your analysis directly depends on the accuracy of your sources, which means that you must carefully verify your source material to the fullest extent possible. If your analysis is based entirely on newspaper sources and Wikipedia articles, the reality is that you will have no idea whether any of it is actually true. It is not information that you can vouch for. As much of your analysis as possible should contain information that you know, for a fact, to be correct. The process is very similar to a law enforcement officer trying to build a case: the case is solid only if the officer knows that the source material is legitimate. Over time, an analyst, like a law enforcement officer, will develop a good overview of the sources and be able to more easily and effectively discern which ones are trustworthy and which ones are not.

For instance, staying with our al-Shabaab example, a newspaper may mention that Somalia has the lowest GDP per capita in East Africa and explain that this fact is somehow significant to al-Shabaab's ability to recruit. Do not simply take that information at face value. Go to World Bank or IMF publications to verify that statement before you make it a part of your product, and cite the primary source. The difference is crucial because the World Bank and IMF are authorities on matters of national economy, while your newspaper reporter is not. If this particular aspect of your analysis becomes important, you will now be able to vouch for the figure you use in your analysis because you have yourself verified it. This allows you to own your analysis in an entirely different way than if you merely regurgitate what other analysts and writers have already said.

When handling sources you need to, without exception, be aware of biases. This applies to the sources you use for context, but also to a specific speech or interview that you may be trying to analyze within that context. Often, material reaches the analyst after multiple layers of bias have been added to it. Say, for instance, that a Hamas leader gives a speech. That speech is then published in a Palestinian newspaper, which in turn is commented on in an Israeli newspaper, and is then picked up by a U.S. news outlet. At every stage, the speech is liable to "change" somehow; some level of bias may be imposed upon it that may distort the original context, the speaker's intentions, and even his words. By the time the speech reaches the analyst, he or she may have no idea about any of this, believing that the quotes and context given in the U.S. edition are straight from the source. Some biases are more apparent than others, but they all matter because they interfere with the analyst's ability to gain insight into, and accurately interpret, the original primary source. All primary source material should be verified as far as possible; the closer to the original source, the better.

Words not only have meaning, but also purpose—sometimes several purposes. This is true also for acts of terrorism: a particular bomb attack may be designed to send one message to the group's constituency or ingroup, another message to competing terrorist groups, and yet another message to its enemy and their constituency. By knowing the target audience and the occasion and placing these in the wider contexts described earlier, we can know something about the subtext and purpose of a specific attack, speech, or interview. It may indicate future plans, burgeoning alignments, or potential vulnerabilities not previously understood. Listed below are some distinctions that matter for analysis. It is important to note that almost any combination of these variables is possible, and it is the task of the analyst to think critically about all of them.

Is the intended audience…

- the ingroup or the outgroup?
- core members or a wider support network?
- enemy leadership or enemy supporters?
- the international community, another terrorist group, or a patron?

Is the occasion…

- a particular celebration (e.g. a military victory or a significant anniversary)?
- a prepared speech or an improvised interview?
- given to a friendly or hostile journalist/news outlet?

If a statement announcing the escalation of terrorist activities is made to a closed session of core ingroup supporters, or is addressed to the enemy leadership during a mass rally, even identically-worded messages could take on very different implications. We know this from everyday party politics at home: a politician will highlight different issues and use different language depending on whether he or she speaks to the party base during a primary election, to top donors during a fundraising dinner, to members of a particular workforce, at a conference of foreign heads of state, in a Sunday morning talk show, or during a televised address to the nation. In each of these, audience and occasion dictates what is being said.

Context and source awareness form a feedback loop: the more you know about the relevant context, the better aware you will be about which sources are useful, which in turn improves your knowledge of the terrorist group or event you seek to analyze, which in turn feeds back into your background knowledge of relevant context. Even though practice may not always make perfect, it does ensure constant improvement.

Analyzing Sources

These are some aspects of source analysis that you'll want to turn a keen eye to in order to detect bias.

Editing: Most apparent may be the way that a text has been edited. If anything has been omitted, it has been omitted for a reason. That reason may be limited column space, but it may also be for political reasons, and all editing impacts content. What is not included may be as important as what is included.

Editorial position: Connected to the editing is the editorial position— the political bias of the source of your text. Does the publication or group from which your source came have a history of slanting stories in a particular way? Editorial positions may affect the context in which a news item is placed, and also what aspects of a story are highlighted, included, or excluded. It is therefore extremely important that the analyst "restores" the original context, chain of events, and intention as much as possible.

Your own biases: Your own bias is as important as the bias of the source when approaching the material. Do you have important connections, loyalties, beliefs, or convictions that affect how you approach the material? If so, how? In order to produce optimal analysis, you need to account for your biases so that you can balance against them. Failing to do so will skew your product and achieve nothing more than adding yet another layer of bias.

Looking for the audience and the occasion: If you are looking at a transcript of a speech or address by a terrorist, to whom were the remarks originally directed, and why? This matters because the composition of the intended audience and the occasion on which they are addressed affect both the form and content of what is actually said. The form and content of a speech to ingroup members following a military victory is going to be different from the form and content of an interview given to a U.S. cable TV station, which will be different again from an address given to an international political conference.

Working through Examples

 An article published in The Mark News, an independent news website that publishes opinion pieces by "global newsmakers on topics of international significance."

The article below is by influential terrorism analyst Brian Jenkins. It is an insightful piece on the public break between al-Qaeda Central and its affiliate, the Islamic State of Iraq and the Levant (ISIL). Jenkins' writing is the kind of secondary analytical source that you might want to access, contextualize, and make use of as you prepare your own analysis for a decision maker. Using our SIT analytical framework and other markers, we will break down portions of this article as an example of how his text can be organized and contextualized, maximizing our information yield while maintaining the analytical rigor needed to present decision makers with coherent and defensible advice. These tools compel the analyst to take seriously the nuances within the organization and the importance of geographic, national, theological, and political frames, where many may see only an undifferentiated mass of Islamic terrorist bickering.

> *Faced with open defiance from the leader of al-Qaeda's affiliate in Syria and Iraq, al-Qaeda leader Ayman al-Zawahiri publicly expelled the Islamic State of Iraq and the Levant (ISIL), suspending its franchise and stripping it of its status as part of the al-Qaeda global enterprise. The split will test the value of al-Qaeda's brand.*[1]

---

1   Brian Michael Jenkins, "Discord Among Terrorists", http://www.themarknews.com/2014/02/24/discord-among-terrorists/ (accessed 2-26-14).

- In this short paragraph we see information contrary to the common assumption that local groups commonly identified as al-Qaeda (AQ) affiliates always seek the approval and status of AQ Central. In a patron-client context, the affiliate's local issues may outweigh the benefit AQ Central can give them. If we are studying AQC, what other local affiliates around the world may have local concerns that outweigh loyalty to their central organization?

- The paragraph also exemplifies the dynamic and ever-changing context in which terrorist groups operate.

- The insubordination of the ISIL and the punitive counter-measures by AQC are clearly part of a negative challenge-response exchange.

- The relationship to AQC, previously perceived to be a benefit to ISIL, is now seen as negative by those within the group.

- The ISIL demonstrates that local context is the most important factor to them.

- In short, the context of the group in relation to AQ Central has changed and counter terrorism practitioners have an opportunity to reevaluate our relationship to that group to see if there is an action or policy advantage we can gain from recognizing that the group and its context have changed.[2]

> *Although al-Qaeda's leaders have quarreled in the past over strategy, tactics, and targets, an open break like this is unprecedented and creates real risks for the leadership of both organizations. So what's next?* [2]

- If the ISIL has lost its patron, will it now seek new a new patron and new allies?

- Given its ideological and theological commitments, as well as its goals on the ground, what groups are likely to be new partners?

---

2   Ibid.

- What was the cause of this split? Knowing the answer may tell us something about possible new patrons and partners.

- Is this group transitioning in a way that can be framed and used to our advantage?

Al Qaeda's leaders place great importance on maintaining unity.

> *The rebellious ISIL is not likely to dissolve itself, and ISIL leader Abu Bakr al-Baghdadi—who has already rejected Zawahiri's orders, claiming that he obeys only God—seems unlikely to back down. Now that al-Qaeda has declared ISIL a renegade, however, its leaders cannot allow ISIL to succeed in creating a rival center of power. That sets up a showdown that could turn an internal dispute into a schism that cuts across the jihadist universe.*[3]

- The description of the conflict over patronage is a question of who will be viewed as the patron to jihadists in general. By rejecting Zawahiri's orders—in effect claiming that these orders are contrary to God's will—the centerpiece becomes conflict with, rather than devotion to, AQC.

- Al-Baghdadi's challenge to Zawahiri's patronage reflects the ISIL's internally coherent but different interpretation of what it means to "obey God." The group's understanding of obedience to God is central to its perception of itself as coherent, and to how it operates in its specific geographic context.

- This negative honor challenge between AQ and the ISIL suggests the possibility for more nuanced openings and the need for policy maneuvers that are able to deal with the new situation on the ground.

---

3   Ibid.

2 An article written by Tony Sayegh published in *The Palestinian Pundit,* a blog described as a "site for analysis of Palestinian politics and the posting of relevant articles."

In "Does this Make Sense to You?" journalist Tony Sayegh critiques Palestinian insistence on statehood, asking whether or not the implications of that policy is realistic, furthers the agenda of the Palestinian National Movement, or whether it even makes sense. He pinpoints a number of decisions and behaviors that are frequently brought up to show that Palestinian behavior is irrational, unpredictable, or simply self-destructive. Applying SIT and the cultural markers we have learned in this book, however, we can see that these behaviors themselves give us additional insight into Palestinian perceptions and agendas.

> *... it is easier to pin down, immobilize and defeat the forces and institutions of a state than to build a state... So, why are the Palestinians who do not have a state in reality want to pretend that they have one? Why are they burdening themselves with the trappings of a state when these are not assets, but liabilities? So you have a 'parliament' that can't convene because half of its members have been arrested. You have an 'executive force' that is patrolling streets and street corners making for easy targets for the Israelis; what is the point?* [4]

The point, according to SIT, is to enhance the status and social identity of members and supporters, thereby boosting their commitment to the group and its struggle. Statehood may be an inconvenient part of the armed struggle, but it is essential for positive social identities. The Palestinians are in conflict with the State of Israel and do not want to be perceived as an inferior party, which would entail

---

4   Article dated 04/29/2007, accessed online 02/27/2014 at http://palestinianpundit.blogspot. com/2007/04/does-this-make-sense-to-you.html.

a negative social identity, despondency, loss of support, and thereby a weakening of the struggle. They want to be seen as politically legitimate by the international community because international recognition is a further source of positive social identity. For this reason, then, they need to be democratic, which means that parliamentary rule is an essential part of their claim to legitimate statehood.

Also, the Executive Force patrols the streets to demonstrate to the people that the Palestinian movement has gone from stateless guerrillas to statehood; that the movement is making progress, and that it is thus as a source of positive social identification. Moreover, from a Palestinian perspective, when Israelis arrest members of Palestinian National Assembly and prevent the cabinet from meeting, it is a testament to Israel's failure to accept the rules of national statehood. According to the challenge-response model, this should, in Palestinian eyes, bring not only Palestinian and regional Arab disapproval of Israel, but ought also to cause the international community to withdraw their support of Israel.

Sayigh continues by comparing the situation in Palestine to other conflict zones, pointing out certain similarities and asking why the Palestinians are so insistent on statehood (even if in name only) when the drawbacks and risks are so obvious.

Look at Iraq, Afghanistan and more recently Somalia. These are examples of 4GWs [Fourth Generation Wars] where the guerrilla is fighting the forces of a puppet state supported by an occupying power. We have the same situation in occupied Palestine: the PA is an extension of the occupation and it is propped up by the occupier and by the U.S.; why pretend otherwise? Are the U.S. and Israel not arming and training the PA forces? For what purpose? Are the Israelis and Americans not coordinating 'security' with the PA? For what purpose? [5]

---

5   Ibid.

To begin, the situation in Palestine is not the same as the ones in Iraq, Afghanistan, or Somalia. SIT requires us to be sensitive to differences in cultural, geographical, and socioeconomic context from place to place and case to case. Each armed conflict has a combination of contexts that may be similar, but almost never identical. The Palestinians, as opposed to the Iraqis or Somalis, have been struggling for independent statehood for more than half a century. To them, the symbolism and status of statehood have a different impact on the conflict than these other places. Also, while it is true that the PA under Arafat became a mere tool of Israeli policy, it is also true that when Hamas formed a cabinet after its January 2006 landslide victory, it refused to accept the validity of the "treasonous" treaties and accords with Israel made by the previous government. This was a challenge against Israel, but also against Arafat's Fateh party. The response was a coordinated effort (together with the U.S. and EU) to bring down the Palestinian government. The public evaluation of that response led to increased popular support for Hamas, which was seen as having done the honorable thing despite the risk involved. Challenge and response was followed by public assessment, and it was in favor of the apparent loser.

3   An article written by Charles Krauthammer published in NY Daily News, the 4th most widely-distributed daily newspaper in the United States.

Pundits and journalists are often keen to have their readers adopt their analysis of an event, presenting their context of choice emphatically and to the exclusion of alternative or even complementary contextual layers. This is particularly problematic when the pundit in question is a knowledgeable, respected, and persuasive writer; a reader's impulse may be to simply accept what is presented and incorporate it into his or her own analysis. Nevertheless, analysts must always question the contexts and conclusions offered to them. As noted above, an analyst cannot fully own analysis that is only partially his or her own product. With that in mind, consider this statement by renowned security affairs commentator Charles Krauthammer:

> *The advent of suicide bombing coincides precisely with the era of Israeli conciliation and attempts at peacemaking. It is precisely in the context of the most accommodating, most conciliatory, most dovish Israeli policy in history that the suicide bombings took hold.*[6]

While an important point is made here, is "dovish Israeli policy" the only background against which Hamas' introduction of suicide bombings should be understood? Are there other layers of context that, when brought into play, will provide a more nuanced and realistic perspective? What does Hamas have to say about context? Remember, being able to balance the Emic and Etic perspectives of a situation is the foundation for good analysis.

> *Hamas declared itself in 1987 and it stated clearly that its military action was directed against the military forces of the Zionist entity, not at civilian people either inside or outside Palestine. But every day the Zionists were killing our women and children, destroying our houses and cutting down our trees. After the attack against the Ibrahimi Mosque… Hamas decided that it had no choice but to repay the Zionists in kind.*[7]

When Hamas introduced suicide operations, it was against the background of ongoing Palestinian civilian casualties on the ground which, in the eyes of ordinary Palestinians (Hamas' primary constituency and recruitment

---

6   Editorial, *New York Daily News,* 03/27/2002 (http://www.nydailynews.com).
7   Anders Strindberg, "Interview with Imad al-'Alami" (Damascus, November 2001), *Jane's Intelligence Review,* vol. 13, no. 11 (November 2001), p. 64.

base), contrasted sharply against the Israel's stated "dovish" policy. Specifically, in February 1994, Baruch Goldstein, a U.S.-born resident of the Kiryat Arba settlement in Hebron, used an assault rifle to open fire on worshippers at the Ibrahimi Mosque, killing twenty-nine and wounding 125 before being overpowered and killed himself. According to Hamas, this event, which a Hamas cadre later described as "the first suicide attack in the history of the Palestinian-Zionist conflict," brought a turning point in the organization's tactics. Emic accounts must also be verified, and can never be taken at face value. In this case, the timeline matches up to the claim. Like the other Palestinian factions, prior to the Hebron massacre, Hamas had engaged primarily in drive-by shootings, stabbings and car bombings, distinguishing itself only by the frequency of its attacks. Following the massacre, the organization introduced the tactic of suicide operations inside Israel, irrevocably changing the face of the conflict. This is, of course, only one of a number of possible frames. Additionally, the analyst must examine Krauthammer's claim, the impact of regional events, pressures from state sponsors, conflict with other Palestinian groups that might have called for some action that distinguishes the ingroup from the various outgroups, and so forth. The main point is that there is almost never only one frame that is relevant for analysis of any social phenomenon, including terrorism and terrorist attacks. The analyst must place an event such as this within the context of the group's own understanding of its actions and context, and balance that against other factors that emerge as significant. Just like other sources, the terrorists' self-understanding and presentation of their actions have to be verified, contextualized, corroborated, and scrutinized as far as it is possible. They are no less likely to engage in spin than anyone else, but their perspective is nevertheless an important part of the analytical puzzle.

A status update from the Facebook page of the Animal Liberation Front (ALF). This social media presence is for recruiting and public support purposes.

In an effort to show how ingroup and outgroup dynamics work in the challenge-response cycle, we have used statements taken from the Facebook page of the ALF.[8] The SIT framework and analytical markers can be used to organize and highlight the sometimes subtle differences between groups within what many assume is a homogenous animal rights movement.

The ability to influence public opinion and gain public support is considered a limited good (which you will remember is a limited resource that cannot be shared—"your gain, my loss") by many or most substate violent movements. Framing the discussion below—in which ALF is vying for the ability to influence opinion with two other major animal rights organizations—as challenge and response centered on a limited good allows us to see the dynamic behind the statements.

 Animal Liberation Worldwide
2 days ago

In the last decade, for instance, PETA pressured McDonalds, Burger King, and KFC to increase cage size and adopt 'less cruel and more profitable' slaughter methods,[1] while Humane Society of the United States (HSUS) aggressively campaigned for 'humane meat' and 'cage-free eggs.

8   https://www.facebook.com/search/web/?q=animal%20liberation%20 front&form=FBFASA&sid=0.7119160343427211&source=ta.

In this post ALF sets the scene for animal rights activists that are deciding what form of activism they will join. Big corporations in general, and fast food chains in particular, are seen as outgroups by animal rights activists. ALF presents PETA and the Humane Society of the United States as having made a positive honor challenge toward this easily recognized outgroup. That difference is a distinction that ALF can build upon further to separate their ingroup—"those who do something"—from "those who talk." Commitment to action on behalf of animals is a baseline honorable position, and is perceived and evaluated by animal rights activists in the contest for support.

Animal Liberation Worldwide
17 hours ago

These groups ultimately serve corporate exploiters' interests and champion capitalist principles generally.

This post moves beyond pointing out that PETA and HSUS have failed to act in opposition to the outgroup; they now make significant negative honor challenges against them. Those who are predisposed to view fast food and big business (and indeed capitalism in general) negatively and outside their animal rights ingroup are now presented with a stark choice: those described as collaborating with the enemy or those who are willing to take action (ALF) on behalf of animals.

Animal Liberation Worldwide
10 hours ago

But whereas PETA began as a grassroots organization in 1980 and continues to defend the Animal Liberation Front (ALF) and to promote veganism, HSUS has been a bureaucratic welfare group since its inception in 1954, it consistently denounces the ALF, and has always capitulated to carnivorous culture as it barely gives support even for vegetarianism.

In this final post the analyst can see the patronage ALF believes, or wants the reader to believe, that it exercises over PETA. The sentence makes clear that although PETA does not go as far as in its activism as ALF believes one should, PETA nevertheless defends ALF's actions as ethical. HSUS, meanwhile, is presented as aligned with bureaucracy and government—an outgroup that has not (from ALF's perspective) taken adequate actions to protect animals.

These three posts from the Animal Liberation Front's Facebook page provide insight into who is and who is not likely to support ALF's illegal actions, why there is a split in the animal rights movement, and on what grounds. It shows succinctly why it would be a mistake to consider the animal rights movement as a monolith, and why specific counter-measures and policies must target specific groups, while perhaps reaching out to other groups. On the face of it, it may seem simply straightforward: group A does not like group B and engages in verbal attacks. So what? Well, by placing even such simple observations within the SIT framework and against the background of the analytical markers, our observation automatically yield two additional things: a set of assumptions that tell us about the dynamics of this enmity, and a set of questions with which to move forward. Remember, facts are the basic building blocks and the framework is the scaffolding that guides and gives shape to your analytical product.

5 A string of tweets from August Kreis' Twitter account. Kreis uses Twitter to communicate his messages to those within his ingroup, as well as to make negative honor challenges against outgroups.

August Kreis III is a neo-Nazi, Identity theology adherent, KKK member, and neo-Constitutionalist. In 1999 he joined the Aryan Nations and, when Richard Butler died, he fought for control of the organization.[9] Kreis is perhaps most famous (or infamous) for trying to contact al-Qaeda during an interview on CNN.[10]

SIT and our other markers are helpful for understanding the dynamics of Kreis' communications. For instance, Kreis uses Twitter to communicate his ideological and theological message to fellow extremists as well as to those who reject and counter his message. Even brief sentences can be exploited and mined in order to produce analytical insights. Below is an exchange in which "Matthew" (we have removed his last name) challenges some of Kreis' assertions, suggesting that Kreis must be taking his position from Jewish rather than Christian tradition—something Matthew is aware will make Kreis angry.[11]

---

9   "Posse leader joins Aryan World Congress," *Spokane Spokesman-Review,* July 15, 2000.
10 "An unholy alliance: Aryan Nation leader reaches out to al Qaeda", CNN. 2005-03-29. (accessed 09-25-2007).
11 https://twitter.com/ABKreis3.

Tweets

Matthew X @ MatthewXXX • 13 Mar 2012

Is that from the Talmud? My Catholic faith doesn't recognize that as a tradition.

August B. Kreis III @ABKreis3 • 13 Mar 2012

Deu 23:2 A bastard shall not enter into the congregation of the LORD; even to his tenth generation shall he not enter into ....

In his response to Matthew, Kreis asserts his ingroup credentials and bases his response on the authority of Christian Old Testament text, (Deuteronomy 2:23). Kreis disregards the obvious reality that his Christian text is also sacred text to Jews—the ultimate outgroup in Kreis' worldview. Kreis' hermeneutic position and his follow-up interpretation becomes extremely important because Kreis has set himself up as singularly authoritative. While the text may be interpreted differently by those outside his ingroup using another hermeneutic framework, Kreis' frame is essential to the way he understands his own authority.

Tweets

August B. Kreis III @ABKreis3 • 13 Mar 2012

Not from the kike talmud it's from the Holy Parchments. A Mamzer is a bastard of mixed race heritage

---

As the exchange continues, Kreis takes up the question of where one of his religious beliefs is found. He disregards the fact that the concept being discussed—mamzer, a person born as a result of illicit relations—is indeed defined in the Babylonian Talmud, as well as other Jewish legal sources (although not as a mixed race person, but as someone born from adultery or incest). Since his theology does not recognize the authority of Jewish texts, his response explains through a negative honor challenge against Judaism that he believes racially-mixed people exist outside of salvation. The short sentences are designed to highlight his embrace of white racial purity as an honorable position, while simultaneously attempting to shame Jews, non-whites, and anyone who does not hold his position. Even the way in which he Kreis capitalizes or fails to capitalize various words are an indication of his ingroup affiliation. "Talmud" is not capitalized (though by tradition it should be), while "Holy Parchments," a reference to his accepted holy text, is capitalized. Finally, the derogatory term "kike" further distances him from his ultimate outgroup, Jews.

Twitter comments are short and often overlooked in research. It is assumed that they are superficial soundbites. While this may be true, even soundbites are written in context; they are instances of communication that can tell us much about the assumptions and world views of those who tweet. Having an adaptable yet robust analytical framework allows us to organize and use even these short statements to further elucidate our understanding of a person, a group, or an ideological position.

Living with change

Analysts need to recognize that terrorism, terrorist groups, and terrorists are, like all social phenomena and agents, subject to development and change. Terrorists tend to be "change agents": they seek, through violence, to alter the social or political status quo in some way, which requires them to be responsive to their environment. Additionally, terrorist groups themselves change, sometimes to the point that their core ideas and methods are no longer the same as they were originally.

It is often difficult or distasteful for those engaged in counter terrorism to accept a view of terrorism as fluid. Nevertheless, analysts must be prepared to take into account the reality of change, and analyze facts as they evolve, in their evolving contexts, wherever that leads. To that end, we must regularly revisit our analyses and test their endurance: what may serve as a very insightful analysis of a terrorist group today may become outdated at any time and for a range of reasons, depending on developments within the group or in the environment within which it operates. The idea that terrorists never change—that the tiger never changes his stripes—is common, but inaccurate.

Consider, for instance, Arafat and his Fateh movement's entry into the Oslo Process. Originally a non-state/substate entity aligned with a number of terrorist organizations and locked in a conflict with Israel, it went on to form the core of a proto-state entity, became party to a formal peace accord with Israel, and was attacked—politically and militarily—by its former allies. Literally from one week to the next, vast segments of the context for evaluating Arafat and his organization changed radically. Factors that seemed crucially relevant in late August 1993 were rendered defunct or turned on their head by mid-September; an analyst seeking to provide insight into Fateh's actions based on the previous month's alignments and known objectives would have been led far astray.

Typically, changes happen more slowly and are not nearly as dramatic. Sometimes, groups and individuals classified as terrorists decide to abandon terrorism altogether. The transformation toward legitimacy requires the terrorist group to no longer see itself as a clandestine organization in opposition to a government, but rather as a legitimate part of the system and therefore unable to accept violent opposition. A case in point: the United States listed the African National Congress (ANC) of South Africa as a Foreign Terrorist Organization until 1990. The reasons for this included: the extended terrorist campaign conducted by the ANC's military wing, Umkhonto we Sizwe (MK); its links to other terrorist organizations worldwide; and the support it had received from the Soviet Bloc. The apartheid regime crumbled and in 1993, and Nelson Mandela, a co-founder of MK, became the president of South Africa. The ANC became the ruling party in good standing with the West, and the following year the remnants of MK were integrated into the South African Defense Forces. That is to say, all of the structural and ideological reasons that had framed and given rise to ANC/ MK terrorism were removed. Terrorism was a lens that was no longer relevant to understand the organization.

Actually, one need look no further than extremism in the United States to see similar changes to the contexts and behaviors of terrorist groups. In 1976 the Church of Israel, led by Dan Gayman, fit neatly into the Christian Identity theology category that also framed the worldview of violent organizations such as the Aryan Nations and various KKK groups. These groups fought against and targeted government officials on the basis of theologically based beliefs about society and politics.[12] On July 2, 1976, Gayman was hit in the head by a Missouri Highway patrolman responding to reports of a fight at the group's compound.

---

12 For a more complete overview of Identity Theology, The Church of Israel and this incident, see David W. Brannan, "The evolution of the Church of Israel: Dangerous mutations," *Terrorism and Political Violence*, Volume 11, Issue 3, 1999. pp.106-118.

This innocuous event was a watershed moment in the history of the Church of Israel. Before, Gayman had asserted that the church and its followers needed to actively resist and confront law enforcement and other branches of government. Following this incident, however, Gayman reinterpreted his view of Romans 13, asserting that the group must be "repentant" rather than "rebellious"; that it must not resist authority, waiting for God to act rather than using force themselves. Whether this was brought on by a sincere theological epiphany or by aversion to further physical pain, the important point is that the group was no longer bound by its previous understanding of biblical text. Gayman's encounter caused him to lead his group away from a violent position that has motivated a number of other groups to embrace terrorism.

Some concluding thoughts

For our analysis to remain relevant, we need to recognize not only the structures and relationships a terrorist or extremist organization may form, but also that they are multi-dimensional and dynamic. No piece of primary source information—not even tweets—is so small that we can simply assume that it is useless for analysis.

No one is born knowing how to conduct effective analysis, or knowing how to use the SIT framework and the other analytical markers. It all takes practice. We urge you to apply the skills and framework that you have found here to any text, video, or other sources you come across in your practice; we are surrounded by opportunities to practice and hone these skills. Think through how small groups—not necessarily terrorist groups, but groups in general—operate in relation to each other. You will rather quickly see the patron/client, honor/shame, and challenge/response mechanisms at work. Try to identify the limited good or resource that groups are vying for. By practicing—always keeping an eye open to the structures and dynamics described in this book—you will more easily be able to make similar identifications when you are tasked with analysis of terrorist organizations. One of the benefits of the SIT framework is that it is applicable to any group in a resource-constrained environment; in fact, you can practice using these markers while even looking at your own department, agency, or other government entity.

By using the method and markers outlined in this handbook, you can build your analytical capability. Better analysis makes a better foundation for our operational and policy decisions, which is an important building block in the ongoing effort to improve our homeland and national security.

Chapter Summary:

- Analysis differs from profiles because it takes the facts from a profile and then seeks to interpret them using a particular framework or combination of different, complementary frameworks.

- Contextualization is essential for understanding the issues you seek to analyze. Some contextual factors you might look at include: national/regional politics, theological markers, social and cultural group settings, group objectives, etc.

- Once you learn about contextual issues of a particular group or phenomenon, your future analysis will be partially constructed; all you have to do is add your new findings and adapt your analysis according to the newly-available information.

- When possible, use primary sources, and know that the savvy analyst will become better at determining valuable source material as he or she gains more experience and insight.

- While you can never eliminate bias from your work or your sources, it is important that you are aware of it in order to ensure the most accurate interpretation possible.

- To locate bias in your sources, look at the way a text has been edited, the text's editorial position, your own biases, the intended audience, and the occasion.

- SIT and the other analytical markers you have been introduced to in this book can be used to examine sources as various as newspaper articles, Twitter posts, blog posts, and Facebook status updates, as well as academic sources.

References & Additional Resources

General Terrorism

Robert M. Entman, *Projections of Power*, (Chicago, University of Chicago Press, 2004).

Christopher Hewitt, *Understanding Terrorism in America: From the Klan to al-Qaeda* (London and New York: Routledge, 2003).

Philip B. Heymann's, *Terrorism and America: A Commonsense Strategy for a Democratic Society*, (Cambridge: MIT Press, 1998).

Bruce Hoffman, *Inside Terrorism*, (New York: Columbia University Press, 2006).

Paul R. Pillar, *Terrorism and U.S. Foreign Policy*, (Washington, DC: Brookings Institute, 2001).

Andrew T. H. Tan, (Ed.), *The Politics of Terrorism: A Survey*, (London: Routledge, 2006) pp. 3-16.

David Tucker, *Illuminating the Dark Arts of War: Terrorism, Sabotage, and Subversion in Homeland Security and the New Conflict*, (New York: Continuum International Publishing Group, 2012).

Religious Terrorism

Reza Aslan, *Beyond Fundamentalism: Confronting Religious Extremism in the Age of Globalization*, (New York, NY: Random House, 2010).

Mateus Soares De Azevedo, *Men of a Single Book: Fundamentalism in Islam, Christianity, and Modern Thought*, (Bloomington, IN, World Wisdom, 2010).

Jonathan Fox, *Ethnoreligious Conflict in the Late Twentieth Century*, (Lanham, MD: Lexington Books, 2002).

Jonathan Fox, *"Do Religious Institutions Support Violence or the Status Quo?,"* Studies in Conflict and Terrorism, 22:119-139, 1999.

Bruce Hoffman, *"Holy Terror": The Implications of Terrorism Motivated by a Religious Imperative*, (Santa Monica, CA: 1993).

Mark Jeurgensmeyer, *Terror in the Mind of God: The Global Ride of Religious Violence* (Berkley: University of California Press, 2000).

Mark Juergensmeyer and Margo Kitts (ed.), *Princeton Readings in Religion and Violence*, (Princeton, NJ: Princeton University Press, 2011).

Islamism

Scott Appleby (Ed.), *Spokesmen for the Despised: Fundamentalist Leaders of the Middle East*, (Chicago: Chicago University Press, 1996).

John L. Esposito, *The Islamic Threat: Myth or Reality?*, (New York, NY: Oxford University Press, 1995).

Laura Mansfield (Ed.), *His Own Words: A Translation of the Writings of Dr. Ayman al Zawahiri* (n.p.: TLG Publications, 2006).

Vali Nasr, *The Shia Revival: How Conflicts within Islam will Shape the Future*, (New York, NY: W. W. Norton and Company, 2006).

Nicholas Noe (Ed.), *Voice of Hezbollah: The Statements of Sayyed Hassan Nasrallah* (London &New York: Verso, 2007).

Anders Strindberg & Mats Warn, *Islamism* (Cambridge, UK: Polity Press, 2011).

US Extreme Right and Christian Identity Theology

James Aho, *The Politics of Righteousness: Idaho Christian Patriotism*, (Seattle: University of Washington Press, 1990).

Michael Barkun, *Religion and the Racist Right*, (Chapel Hill, NC: The University of North Carolina Press, 1997).

David W. Brannan, *Violence, Terrorism and the Role of Theology: Repentant and Rebellious Christian Identity* at, http://research-repository.st-andrews.ac.uk/handle/10023/342.

Jeffrey Kaplan, *Radical Religion in America: Millenarian Movements from the Far Right to the Children of Noah*, (Syracuse, NY: Syracuse University Press, 1997).

Countering Violent Extremism

Brad Deardorff, *The Roots of Our Children's War* (Williams, CA: Agile Press, 2013).

Clark McCauley & Sophia Moskalenko, *Friction: How Radicalization Happens to Them and Us*, (Oxford, UK: Oxford University Press, 2011).

Psychology of Terrorism

(Ed.'s), Bruce Bongar, et. al., *Psychology of Terrorism*, (Oxford: Oxford University Press, 2007), pp. 13-31.

John Horgan, *"The search for the terrorist personality."* In A. Silke (Ed.), *Terrorists, victims, and society: Psychological perspectives on terrorism and its consequences* (pp. 3-27).

Fathali M. Moghaddam, *Multiculturalism and Intergroup Relations: Psychological Implications for Democracy in Global Context*, (Washington, DC: American Psychological Association, 2008).

Fathali M. Moghaddam, *How Globalization Spurs Terrorism: The Lopsided Benefits of "One World" and Why That Fuels Violence*, (Westport, CT: Praeger Security International, 2008).

Fathali M. Maghaddam, *From the Terrorist' Point of View: What the experience and why they come to destroy*, (Westport, Connecticut: Praeger Security International, 2006).

(Ed.s), Werner G.K. Stritzke, et.al., *Terrorism and Torture: An Interdisciplinary Perspective*, (Cambridge, UK: Cambridge University Press, 2009).

Seth J. Schwartz, Curtis S. Dunkel, and Alan S. Waterman, *"Terrorism: An Identity Theory Perspective,"* in *Studies in Conflict and Terrorism*, Volume 32, # 6, June 2009, pp. 537-559.

Suicide Terrorism

Peter Chalk and Bruce Hoffman, *The Dynamics of Suicide Terrorism: Four Case Studies of Terrorist Movements*, (Santa Monica, CA: RAND, 2005).

Bruce Hoffman, David W. Brannan, Eric Herren and Robert Matthiessen, *Preparing for Suicide Terrorism: A Primer for American Law Enforcement Agencies and Officers* (Santa Monica, CA: RAND, 2004).

Ami Pedahzur, *Suicide Terrorism*, (Malden, MA: Polity Press, 2005).

Terrorism Analysis

David W. Brannan, Philip F. Esler and N.T. Anders Strindberg, *"Talking to Terrorists: Towards an Independent Analytical Framework for the Study of Violent Substate Activism,"* in, Studies in Conflict and Terrorism, Volume 24, #1, January/February 2001, pp. 3-24.

Ian O. Lessor et. al., *Countering the New Terrorism*, (Santa Monica, CA: RAND, 1999) pp. 39-84.

Richard K. Betts, *"How to Think About Terrorism,"* in *The Wilson Quarterly*, p.4 accessed 3-10-10 at, http://www.columbia.edu/cu/siwps/publication_files/betts/How%20to%20Think%20About%20Terrorism%20-%20Betts.pdf.

Seth G. Jones and Martin C. Libicki, *How Terrorist Groups End: Lessons for Countering al Qa'ida*, (Santa Monica, CA: RAND, 2008).

Critical Thinking

Richard L. Epstein, *The Pocket Guide to Critical Thinking* (Socorro, NM: Advanced Reasoning Forum, 2011).

bell hooks, *Teaching Critical Thinking: Practical Wisdom*, (New York, NY: Routledge, 2010).

Sociology, Anthropology, and Social Identity Theory

W. G. Austin and S. Worchel (Ed.'s), *The social psychology of intergroup relations*, (Monterey, CA: Brooks/Cole, 1979).

Peter Berger and Thomas Luckmann, *The Social Construction of Reality*, (London, UK: Penguin Books, 1966).

Peter Berger, *The Sacred Canopy: Elements of a Sociological Theory of Religion*, (New York, NY: DoubleDay, 1967).

Rupert Brown, *Group Processes: Dynamics within and between Groups* (Oxford: Basil Blackwell, 1988).

Manuel Castells, *The Power of Identity*, (Oxford, UK: Blackwell Publishers Ltd, 1997).

Philip F. Esler, *Galatians* (London: Routledge, 1998).

David D. Gilmore (ed.), *Honour and Shame and the Unity of the Mediterranean* (Washington, DC: American Anthropological Association, 1987)

Michael A. Hogg and Dominic Abrams, *Social Identifications: A Social Psychology of Intergroup Relations and Group Processes* (London and New York: Routledge, 1988).

Bruce J. Malina, *The New Testament World: Insights from Cultural Anthropology*, (Louisville, KY: Westminster/John Knox Press, 1993).

J. G. Peristiany (Ed.), *Honour and Shame: The Values of Mediterranean Society* (London: Weidenfeld & Nicolson, 1965).

Julian Pitt-Rivers (ed.), *Mediterranean Countrymen: Essays in the Social Anthropology of the Mediterranean* (Paris and La Haye: Mouton & Co, 1963).

Donatella Della Porta and Mario Diani, *Social Movement: An Introduction*, (Oxford, UK: Blackwell, 1999).

Henri Tajfel, *Differentiation Between Social Groups: Studies in the Social Relations of Intergroup Relations* (London et alibi: Academic Press, 1978).

Henri Tajfel, *Human Groups & Social Categories: Studies in Social Psychology*, (Cambridge, UK: Cambridge University Press, 1981).

Henri Tajfel (Ed.), *Social Identity and Intergroup Relations* (Cambridge et alibi: Cambridge University Press, 1982; first paperback edition 2010).

Stella Ting-Toomey, *Communicating Across Cultures*, (New York, NY: The Guilford Press, 1999).

Max Weber (trans. H. P. Secher), *Basic Concepts in Sociology* (London, UK: Peter Owen, 1962).

About the Authors

David Brannan, Ph.D., worked on terrorism and insurgency at the RAND Corporation for five years before taking up his current position, teaching at the Naval Postgraduate School's Center for Homeland Defense and Security, in Monterey, CA. While at RAND, he was seconded by the Department of Defense to be the Director of Security Policy in the Iraqi Ministry of Interior under the Coalition Provisional Authority. He is a former southern California SWAT officer. He earned his PhD at the University of St. Andrews, Scotland, where he was a Research Associate in the Center for the Study of Terrorism and Political Violence.

Kristin Darken, M.A., is co-founder and Creative Director at Agile Research & Technology, an educational solutions company focused on research and analysis, and development of educational experiences for analysts and practitioners in the National Security domain. She has over a decade of experience in the effective design and delivery of educational material, collaborating with and supporting faculty and students at the Naval Postgraduate School's Center for Homeland Defense and Security. At the Naval Postgraduate School she helped faculty members translate complex ideas and theoretical content within their courses into significant learning experiences grounded in sound instructional design and learning theory.

Anders Strindberg, Ph.D., teaches at the Naval Postgraduate School's Center for Homeland Defense and Security, Monterey, CA. His PhD from the University of St Andrews, and much of his subsequent field research, has focused on Palestinian, Syrian, and Lebanese politics. He is author of Islamism: Religion, Radicalization, Resistance (with Mats Wärn, Polity Press, 2011). He served as Special Correspondent for Jane's Intelligence Review for six years, reporting from U.N. Headquarters in New York, as well as from Syria and Lebanon, regularly traveling to the region for field research. He has also worked as a consultant on Middle East security issues, primarily with European law enforcement agencies, as well as ministries of defense, foreign affairs, justice, and immigration.

CPSIA information can be obtained
at www.ICGtesting.com
Printed in the USA
FSOW04n0632130416
19078FS